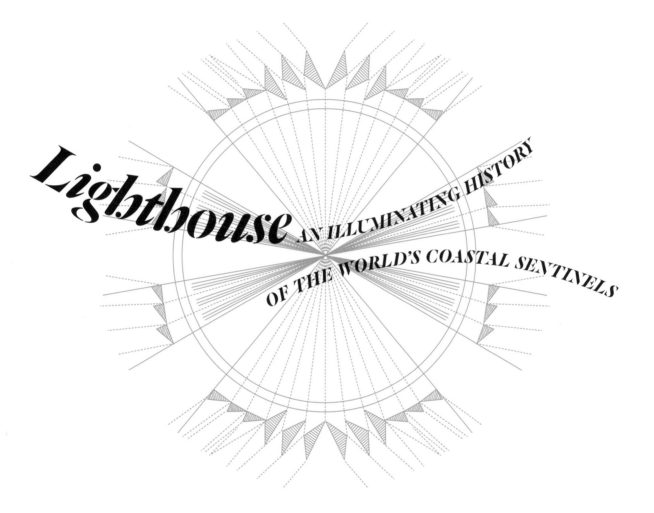

Lighthouse

AN ILLUMINATING HISTORY OF THE WORLD'S COASTAL SENTINELS

R. G. GRANT

BLACK DOG
& LEVENTHAL
PUBLISHERS
NEW YORK

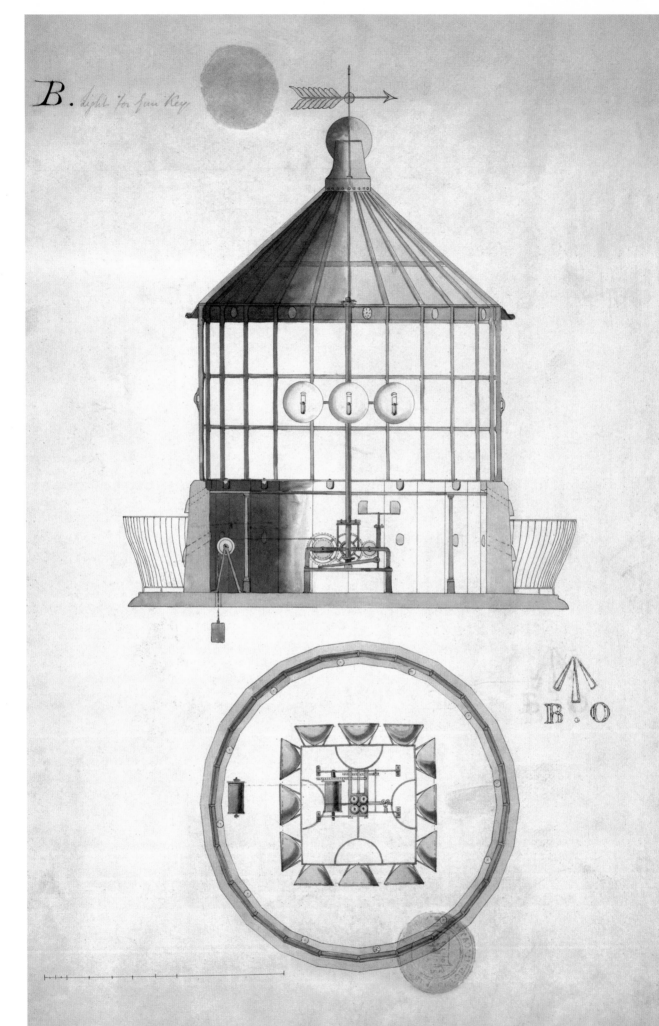

B. Light for Sand Key

B. O

W.O.78/1263/10

C.

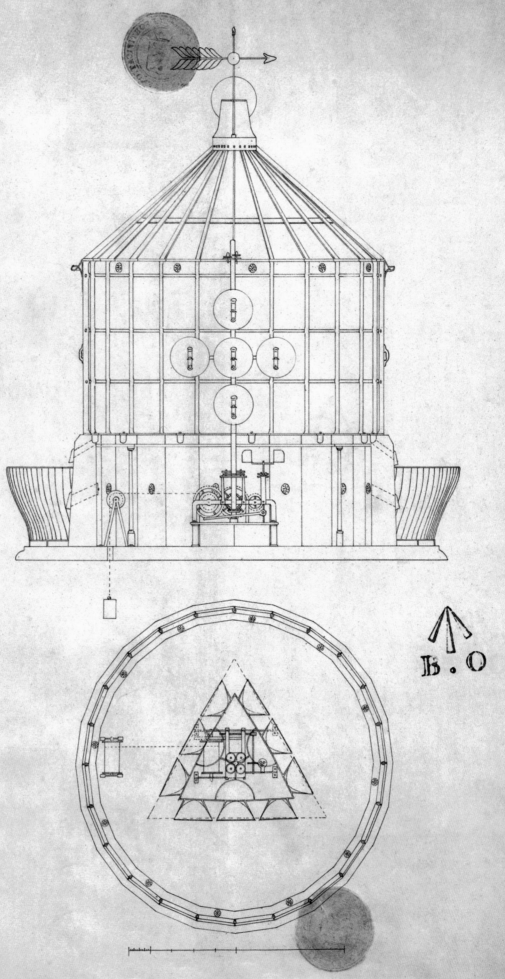

Ь. О

W.O.78/1263/K IV

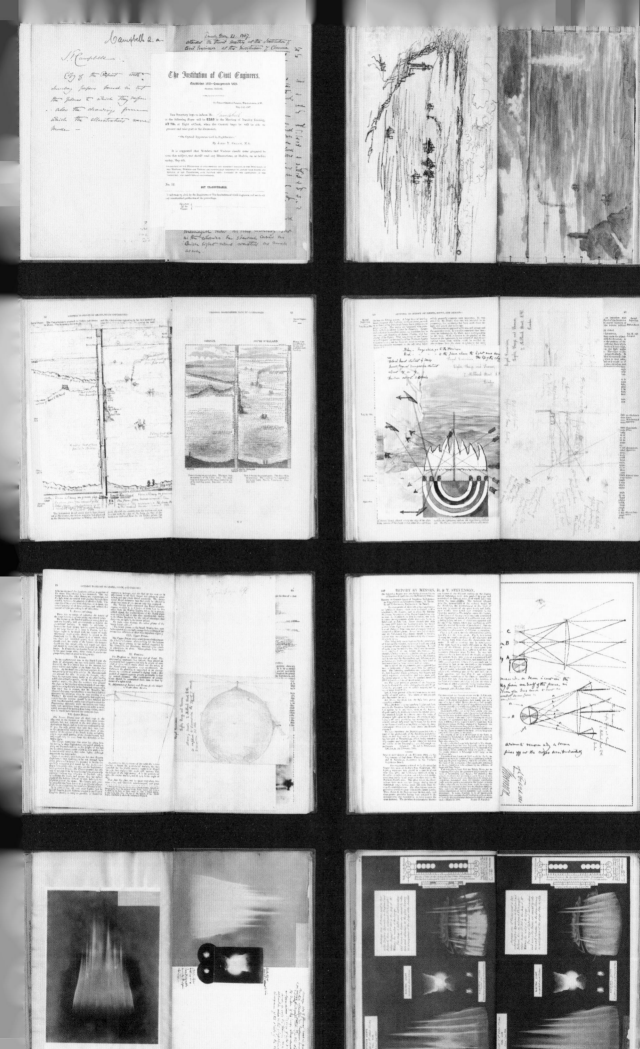

LIGHT KEEPE

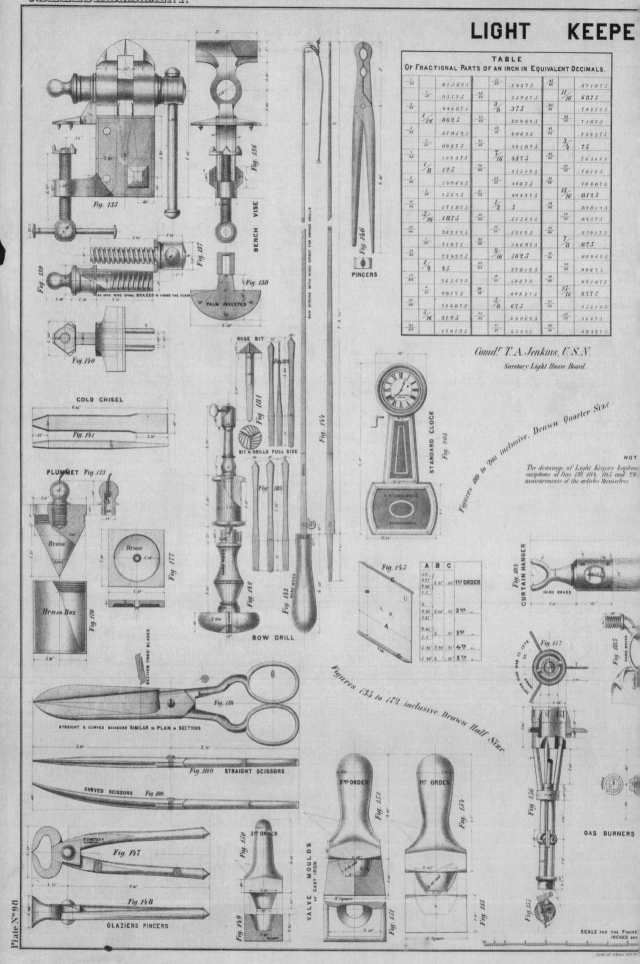

TABLE
OF FRACTIONAL PARTS OF AN INCH IN EQUIVALENT DECIMALS.

Comd'. T. A. Jenkins, U.S.N.
Secretary Light House Board.

NOT
The drawings of Light Keepers Impleme
exceptions of figs. 170, 184, 185 and 20
measurements of the articles themselves

Figures 189 to 200 inclusive. Drawn Quarter Size.

Figures 135 to 172, inclusive. Drawn Half Size.

Fig. 135
Fig. 136 BENCH VISE
Fig. 137
Fig. 138 PALM INVERTED
Fig. 139
AN IRON WIRE SPIRAL BRAZED IN FORMS THE SCREW
Fig. 140

COLD CHISEL
Fig. 141

PLUMMET Fig. 175
Brass
Brass
Fig. 177
Fig. 176
Brass Box

ROSE BIT
Fig. 181
BIT & DRILLS FULL SIZE
Fig. 183
Fig. 182
BOW DRILL
Fig. 144
STEEL
BOW STRING WITH WIRES CUTOUT FOR DRIVING DRILLS

PINCERS
Fig. 146

STANDARD CLOCK
Fig. 205

Fig. 145
A B C
1ST ORDER
2ND
3RD
4TH
5TH

CURTAIN HANGER
Fig. 184
HARD BRASS

Fig. 185
HARD BRASS

Fig. 157
Fig. 156
GAS BURNERS

SECTION THRO BLADES
Fig. 178
STRAIGHT & CURVED SCISSORS SIMILAR IN PLAN & SECTIONS

Fig. 180 STRAIGHT SCISSORS
CURVED SCISSORS Fig. 180

Fig. 147
Fig. 148
GLAZIERS PINCERS

3RD ORDER
Fig. 150
Fig. 149

VALVE MOULDS
OF CAST IRON

2ND ORDER
Fig. 152
Fig. 153

1ST ORDER
Fig. 154
Fig. 155

SCALE FOR THE FIGURE
INCHES and

Lith. of A. Hoen & C° B

IMPLEMENTS.

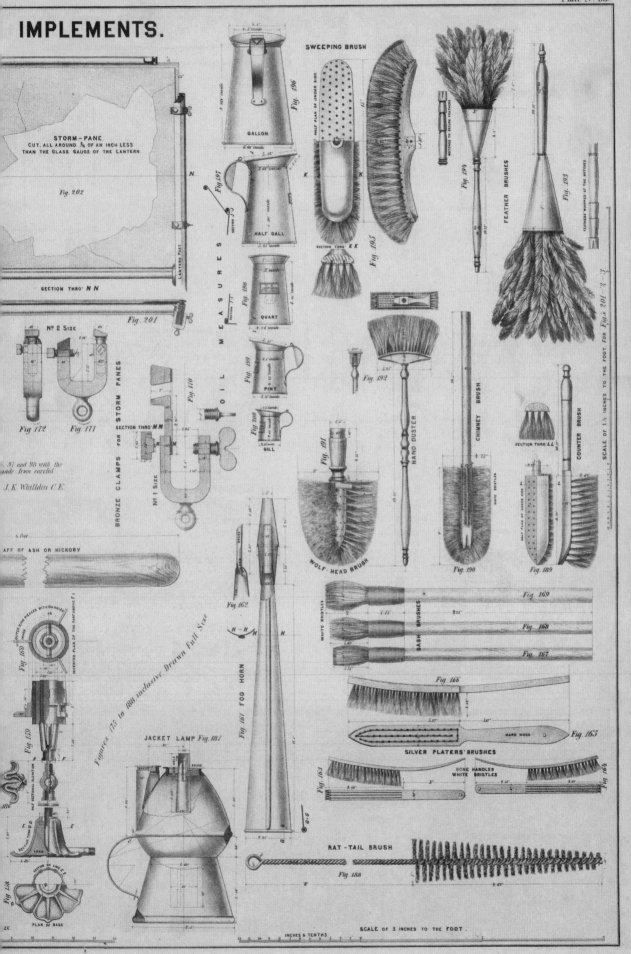

CONTENTS.

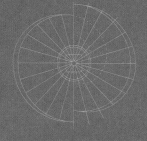
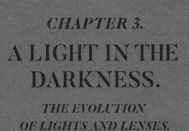

PROLOGUE.

THE

SAGA

OF THE

EDDYSTONE LIGHT.

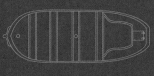

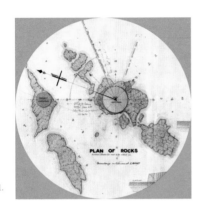

1.

OPPOSITE

Top left: South elevation of Winstanley's original Eddystone lighthouse.

Center left: Horizontal and vertical sections of Smeaton's Eddystone lantern, showing the chandeliers.

Center: Detail from an early 18th-century oil painting by Peter Monamy of Winstanley's first Eddystone.

Center right (top): Detail of an upright section supporting the storeroom at Smeaton's Eddystone.

Center right (center): Upright side and front views of the great tackle from Smeaton's Eddystone, designed to distribute friction as evenly as possible.

Center right (bottom): Detail of the apparatus used to set the cupola on top of the lantern at Smeaton's Eddystone.

Bottom left: Smeaton's Eddystone as it appeared the morning after a storm in 1789.

Bottom right: Detail from an engraving of Winstanley's second Eddystone.

ABOVE

Fig. 1.— A plan of the Eddystone reef, a notorious danger to shipping off the coast of southwest England.

O n Christmas Eve 1695, the merchant ship *Constant*, bound for the port of Plymouth in southwest England, foundered on the rocks of the Eddystone reef. This maritime disaster was, unfortunately, nothing out of the ordinary. Lying off the coast of Devon, the Eddystone had long been recognized as a fearful hazard to shipping, its jagged fingers of rock barely visible above the surface of the ocean, surrounded by swirling seething waters. No one had ever counted the number of ships that were lost there. Indeed, mariners entering the English Channel from the Atlantic sometimes gave the Eddystone such a wide berth that they risked crashing on rocks on the Channel Islands or the north coast of France. The merchants of Plymouth had been granted royal permission for a beacon to be placed on the Eddystone. However, no one could be found to undertake the installation of a light in such a forbidding location. There was simply no precedent for building a lighthouse on offshore rocks.

It so happened that the owner of the ill-fated *Constant* was a most unusual man. Hailing from Saffron Walden in southeast England, Henry Winstanley (1644-1703) was a bold, ambitious entrepreneur with an exceptional talent for mechanical gadgetry. He had turned his Essex home into a public fun palace, and visitors paid handsomely to be entertained by ghostly apparitions, trick chairs, distorting mirrors, and a clockwork organ. A second place of entertainment, his "Waterworks" in London, had as its centerpiece a barrel that dispensed various different drinks on command from the same tap. Winstanley was also a competent engraver and had experience with buildings as clerk of works at Audley End, also in Saffron Walden, one of King Charles II's houses. The profits from an energetic and enterprising life he had invested in five merchant ships. *Constant* was the second of these vessels to be wrecked on the Eddystone, another having foundered there earlier in the same year. Stimulated by this double disaster, Winstanley put himself forward as the man to build a lighthouse on the perilous reef.

The work began in the summer of 1696 and lasted four years. At first it appeared a preposterous undertaking. The only rock on the reef that could support a building presented a sloping surface about half the size of a tennis court. For every day of work, Winstanley and the men he employed spent six hours rowing from Plymouth to the rock and six hours rowing back. The product of the entire first summer's work was twelve holes hacked in the gneiss with picks and a circle of tall iron bars inserted in them. In his *Narrative of the Building*, Winstanley lamented the slow progress due to "the rock being so hard, and the time so short to stay by reason of tides or weather, and the distance from the shore, and the many journeys lost that there could be no landing at all."

During the second summer, a cylindrical stone base was built for the tower, bound to the circle of iron bars. However, the laborious work of transporting huge granite blocks to the construction site was interrupted from an unexpected quarter. The English were, as usual, at war with the French. On June 25, 1697, a French privateer raided the lighthouse building site, kidnapped Winstanley, and carried him back as a captive to France. There he was brought before the Sun King, Louis XIV, who tried to tempt him with an offer of lucrative employment. When this was refused, the king magnanimously ordered that the engineer be sent back to his benevolent labors, commenting loftily that France was "at war with the English, not with humanity."

Throughout the third year of construction, progress was rapid. With a basic structure in place to provide shelter, the workmen could live on the site and therefore put in much longer hours. It was not a comfortable experience. In the worst of the summer weather, they were cut off from contact with the land. As Winstanley wrote, at one point "it was eleven days before any boat could come near us...we were most all the time near drowned with wet...." But up the building went, a wooden octagon rising on the stone base to a height of 60 feet (18 m), topped by a glass-walled lantern and a wrought-iron weather vane, added for decorative effect. On November 14, 1698, Winstanley lit the sixty tallow candles in the lantern. Not a modest man, he asserted that the lighthouse would "stand forever as one of the world's most artistic pieces of work."

Trouble started immediately. For five weeks after the light was lit, Winstanley was trapped on the rock by violent storms. The experience showed he had underestimated the assault the tower would have to withstand. Waves passed fully over the top of the lantern, obliterating the light, and the building shook alarmingly. The engineer's labors were not finished. Beginning in the following spring, he carried out a major rebuild, which included strengthening and raising the entire structure, as well as adding ingenious devices such as cranes

2.

3.

Fig. 2.— Winstanley's first Eddystone lighthouse, accessed by an outside ladder and staircase and topped by an ornamental weather vane.

Fig. 3.— The modified final version of Winstanley's Eddystone light, destroyed in the Great Storm of 1703.

Fig. 4.— Plans of Rudyard's 1709 lighthouse, showing the oak mast at the center of the tower.

ALL OUR WORKS WERE CONSTANTLY BURIED AT THOSE TIMES, AND EXPOSED TO THE MERCY OF THE SEAS.

HENRY WINSTANLEY
c. 1699

4.

to winch up supplies and a chair lift to carry visitors from a boat to the front door. The building was even more ornate than its first incarnation, with many inscriptions on the outer casing and wooden candlesticks protruding from the lantern.

Although there were cynics who carped at this Chinese pagoda in the sea and openly doubted it would last, the building of the Eddystone made Winstanley an admired celebrity. No ship was wrecked on the reef while his tower stood. Unfortunately, that was not for long. In November 1703, with foul weather threatening, Winstanley set off for the Eddystone to effect repairs. In a moment of hubris, he expressed the wish that he might be in the lighthouse through "the greatest storm that ever was." He had his wish. On November 26, southern England was hit by the worst storm in its recorded history, a hurricane that caused thousands of deaths, wrecking buildings, uprooting trees, and flooding the land with a tidal surge. By the time the storm abated the following morning, the lighthouse had disappeared without trace, along with its creator.

Two days after the ruination of Winstanley's light, a merchant ship foundered on the reef with the loss of more than sixty lives. The continued need for an Eddystone lighthouse could not have been demonstrated more starkly. Work on a replacement for Winstanley's tower began in 1706. The man responsible, John Rudyard (or Rudyerd), was a London dealer in silks and other textiles who appears to have had no qualification whatsoever for building a lighthouse. He did, however, have an excellent fund of common sense. Believing that artistic elaboration had been the downfall of the original structure, he envisaged a neat smooth tapering tower with the minimum of protuberances, mounting to a height of 92 feet (28 m). He employed shipwrights from naval dockyards to help create a building that would survive prolonged exposure to the sea. The same pitch-caulked oak planks used to build sailing ships lined Rudyard's lighthouse. There was even a kind of wooden mast raised in the center of the tower.

Rudyard's neat, sensible new Eddystone light successfully went into operation in 1709. Although it was not without problems – its oak planks became worm-eaten and required constant maintenance and replacement – the light of its candles shone for almost half a century before disaster struck again. In the early hours of December 2, 1755, a fire broke out in the lantern room and rapidly spread through the wooden parts of the building. The three keepers fled the inferno and huddled outside until rescued eight hours later. One subsequently died from having ingested molten lead that had dripped from the lantern roof. Of the lighthouse, nothing remained but some heat-twisted iron.

The project to replace Rudyard's lighthouse was pursued with urgency, partly because Britain was once more heading into a war with France (the Seven Years' War began in 1756) and the Royal Navy did not want to risk its fleet running onto an unlighted reef in the English Channel. Yorkshireman John Smeaton (1724-92) was selected for the task. Although it has been said that Smeaton was a strange choice, since he had no experience of architecture or engineering, he could equally be seen as the obvious man for the job. The son of a lawyer, he had followed a natural bent for mechanical invention and established himself in London as a maker of instruments such as pyrometers and navigational devices. He had been elected a Fellow of the Royal Society at a young age and had lectured to that august body on the mathematics underlying the motion of waterwheels and windmills. He was, in fact, a quintessential man of the Enlightenment, like his contemporaries Benjamin Franklin in the United States and the authors of the *Encyclopédie* (1751-65) in France, a member of a liberal elite inspired by an open-minded scientific curiosity and a belief in the beneficent power of practical inventions.

Smeaton took an initial decision of prime importance: he intended to build his entire tower of stone. The fate of Rudyard's lighthouse had amply demonstrated the vulnerability of a wooden structure to fire, and Smeaton also believed that the greater weight of a stone structure would allow it better to survive the prolonged battering of the waves. He claimed to have based the shape of his tower on that of an oak tree, which, he wrote, "is broad at its base, curves inwards at its waist, becomes narrower towards the top." He assembled a team of twenty-four workers, half of whom were stonemasons and half laborers from the Cornish tin mines. Quickly tiring of the time-consuming struggle to travel backward and forward from the mainland to the reef, Smeaton established a floating base for his workers on a herring boat anchored near the rock. Construction began in August 1756.

The plan was for the stone blocks to fit together in an immovable solid mass. Each block in a circular course

5.

6.

Fig. 5.— *Smeaton's stone-built Eddystone lighthouse, which entered service in 1759.*

Fig. 6.— *Inside Smeaton's tower were storerooms, a kitchen, a bedroom, and a light room under the lantern.*

Fig. 7.— *Smeaton's view of the rock and the construction of his stone tower.*

Fig. 8.— *Smeaton's sketches of oaks on which he based the form of the lighthouse.*

Fig. 9.— *Douglass's Eddystone light of 1882 stands alongside the stump of Smeaton's tower.*

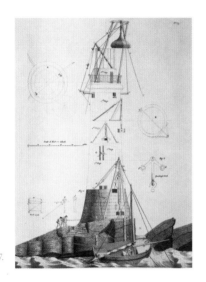

7.

8.

9.

(horizontal layer) of stones was dovetailed to its neighbors with the kind of joint used by carpenters. Marble "joggles" and wooden pins known as "trenails" – the term and the technique borrowed from shipbuilding – connected the courses of stones vertically. All the stone blocks were precisely shaped in a mason's yard on land before being shipped to the rock and hoisted onto the building site using a lifting device of Smeaton's own design. In total, over three years of construction work, some 1,500 blocks were shifted to the Eddystone, with a collective weight of almost 1,000 tons.

In addition to the usual struggle with the wind and waves, Smeaton had to cope with the predations of press gangs, roaming Britain's ports in search of men to conscript forcibly into the country's wartime navy. The engineer obtained official exemption for his workers, but this did not stop them at one point from being pressed en masse and recovered from the navy's hands only with considerable difficulty. Smeaton himself narrowly escaped a freakish death when overcome by fumes from a coke fire lit in an enclosed room of the half-built tower. Discovered in time, he was revived and survived to place a gold ball on top of the cupola – the edifice's sole superfluous decoration – with his own hands. The lighthouse's twenty-four tallow candles were first lit on October 16, 1759. It was not a powerful light by later standards, but Smeaton observed that it shone "very strong and bright to the naked eye" from a distance of 7 miles (11 km).

His fame assured, Smeaton went on to build canals, bridges, and harbors across Britain, in effect founding the profession of civil engineering. Moreover, his lighthouse outlasted the rock on which it was built. By the 1870s, the structure was still sound after standing for more than a century, but wave erosion was opening up a cave in the rock beneath its foundations. As a result, a fourth Eddystone lighthouse had to be built as a replacement, sited on a neighboring rock and designed by engineer James Douglass (1826-98). Lit in 1882, Douglass's Eddystone light stands today alongside the stump of Smeaton's tower. The upper part of the latter was re-erected as a memorial on Plymouth Hoe. It is a piece of history worth preserving, for Smeaton was an inspiration to generations of lighthouse builders who followed in his footsteps. His work laid the foundation for the worldwide system of sea lights that developed over the following century and a half.

CHAPTER I.

WONDERS

OF THE WORLD.

A BRIEF HISTORY

OF THE LIGHTHOUSE.

1.

The story of lighthouses stretches back over two thousand years, to an astonishing structure built on the north coast of Africa in *c.* 280 BC: the Pharos of Alexandria. This was not the first light maintained for the benefit of mariners, but its legendary reputation made it a reference point for every engineer who aspired to lighthouse building into modern times. The Pharos was named for the island on which it was built, a strip of limestone lying off the port of Alexandria on Egypt's Mediterranean coast, linked to the land by a causeway. Traditionally, its architect is said to have been a Greek, Sostratus of Cnidus. However, much that was written about the Pharos in ancient times is so dubious or patently untrue – for example, with regard to the power of its light – that it might be tempting to regard the building as mythical, were it not that level-headed Arab observers were able to describe it still standing more than a thousand years after it was erected and that present-day archaeologists have located its remains at the bottom of the sea.

The most impressive feature of the Pharos was its sheer size. It rose in three sections – a cylinder on top of an octagon on top of a square – to a height of approximately 450 feet (140 m). Few structures were built taller than this until the US skyscraper boom began in the early 20th century. According to the Arab geographer Edrisi, who visited the Pharos in around 1150, it was constructed of white stone blocks held together with lead. The nature of the light at the top of the tower is not known, but whether an open fire or a lantern, its range seems to have been enhanced by a curved mirror. The Pharos was no stripped-down functional building. On the contrary, it was an elaborate monument embellished with statues and sphinxes, no doubt as much an advertisement for the power and wealth of Egypt's rulers, the Ptolemies, as an aid to sailors in finding the harbor mouth. As a prestige building, it proved an undeniable success, for it was acknowledged in antiquity as one of the Seven Wonders of the World (alongside the Great Pyramid of Giza, the Hanging Gardens of Babylon, the Colossus of Rhodes, the Statue of Zeus at Olympia, the Temple of Artemis at Ephesus, and the Mausoleum at Halicarnassus). Its durability was almost as impressive as its size. The Pharos stood largely intact for almost fifteen hundred years, until reduced to ruins by successive earthquakes in 1303 and 1323.

OPPOSITE

Top left: Maplin Sand on the Thames Estuary, the first screw-pile lighthouse ever to be designed.

Top right: Detail of the lighthouse at Spectacle Reef on Lake Huron, its base surrounded by an ice floe.

Center: Detail of Howth Baily, Ireland, where the gas light patented by John R. Wigham was first installed in 1865.

Center right (top): Longstone on Outer Farne; the light could be seen from 20 miles (30 km) away.

Center right (bottom): Engraving depicting the construction of the Héaux de Bréhat lighthouse in France.

Bottom left: Smeaton's Eddystone, after the 1845 addition of a Fresnel lens.

Bottom center: Douglass's design for a railway-mounted movable lantern at the South Stack lighthouse on Anglesey.

Bottom right: Relief depicting the Roman lighthouse at Portus, from the site of ancient Rome's harbor city at Ostia.

ABOVE

Fig. 1.— An artistic impression of the Pharos at Alexandria, one of the Seven Wonders of the Ancient World.

The centuries after the erection of the Alexandrian Pharos saw the triumph of the Roman Empire over an area stretching from the Middle East to Britain. Although the Romans were energetic lighthouse builders, time has erased most evidence of their labors. It is known from ancient texts that an impressive lighthouse once stood at the entrance to Portus, an artificial harbor built on the Italian coast north of Ostia to serve the city of Rome itself. Erected during the reign of Emperor Claudius, who ruled from AD 41 to 54, the lighthouse tower was only a quarter the height of the Alexandrian Pharos, but it was nonetheless an imposing building, fronted by a giant statue of the emperor himself. Yet this ancient glory has disappeared completely, collapsed into the sea, where archaeologists only recently identified a few submerged remains.

In Galicia on the northwest coast of Spain, however, there stands a working lighthouse claiming direct descent from the Roman Empire. The Tower of Hercules light, outside the modern-day town of Coruña, was probably built in the early 2nd century under Emperor Trajan, who ruled from AD 98 to 117. The preserved cornerstone of the building records it as the work of a certain Gaius Sevius Lupus and dedicates it to Mars, god of war. Around the outside of the building, the Roman lighthouse had a spiral ramp, used to carry fuel to the top where a fire provided a light for sailors plying their trade along the treacherous Galician coast. A radical restoration of the tower was completed in 1791, but sufficient elements of the Roman original survive to justify the claim that the Tower of Hercules is the world's oldest functioning lighthouse.

The collapse of Roman rule in Western Europe in the 5th century led to a steep decline in technological skills and social organization. Lights were not maintained and their buildings fell into ruin. European sailors literally entered the Dark Ages. In 810, self-consciously attempting to revive the imperial tradition, Frankish ruler Charlemagne ordered the restoration of the Roman lighthouse at Boulogne on France's northern coast. This structure had been built by the notorious Emperor Caligula on the occasion of his failed bid to invade Britain in c. AD 39, but had since been abandoned. Known as the Tour d'Ordre, the restored Roman building survived until the cliff on which it stood collapsed into the sea in 1644. However, like its English twin – the Roman lighthouse that still stands at Dover on the opposite shore

Fig. 2.— A mosaic representing the 1st-century Roman lighthouse at Portus.

Fig. 3.— The original Tower of Hercules lighthouse in Galicia, Spain, built during the reign of the Roman emperor Trajan.

Fig. 4.— The Lanterna light tower in Genoa, Italy, has stood for almost 900 years.

Fig. 5.— Built on an island in the Baltic, Kõpu lighthouse used a wood fire for illumination.

4.

5.

of the English Channel – the Tour d'Ordre had ceased to function as a beacon long before that time.

Much of the story of medieval European lighthouses has been lost in impenetrable obscurity. This is, perhaps, not surprising because in most cases the lights consisted of little more than a wood fire maintained by monks or a lantern in a church tower. An occasional anecdote surfaces: for example, how French King Louis IX placed a lantern on the Tour de Constance at Aigues-Mortes in southern France, his point of embarkation for his Crusades against the Muslims in 1248 and 1270; or how Walter de Godeton, a landowner on Britain's Isle of Wight, was forced by ecclesiastical pressure to build a light tower at St. Catherine's on the southern tip of the island as a penance for having pilfered monastic wine washed ashore from a shipwreck in 1313. Such examples only serve to emphasize the limited scale of these scattered aids to seafarers.

The revival of Europe's lighthouse-building tradition from its post-Roman collapse began in the maritime city states of Italy. A prime example, the lighthouse known as the Lanterna, was erected to guide ships into the port of Genoa as early as the 12th century. When rebuilt in 1543, this tower attained a height of 250 feet (76 m), or 385 feet (117 m) if the rock on which it stood were included. Like the ancient Alexandrian Pharos, the Lanterna was more than a simple utilitarian aid to navigation, clearly intended to impress every maritime visitor with the wealth and power of the Genoese city state.

The most extensive medieval development of sea lights in northern Europe occurred in the Baltic, where the merchants of the German Hanseatic League pressed for the installation of beacons to facilitate maritime trade. A fire beacon was erected at Falsterbo, then an important trading center at the southern tip of Sweden, as early as the 1220s. Most of the early Baltic lights consisted of no more than a brazier hoisted on a pole, but eventually more substantial lighthouses were constructed. A notable example is the stone-built Kõpu light (also known as Upper Dagerort) on Estonia's Hiiumaa island. Authorized in 1500, the building of Kõpu lighthouse was delayed by war and plague, but eventually a bonfire was lit on top of the stone tower in 1531. Another cluster of medieval sea lights was constructed along the coast of Flanders, reflecting the importance of the Flemish cloth trade. The brick-built fire tower at Nieuwpoort, built in 1284, remained standing until it was blown up during World War I.

In France, the well-known Cordouan tower continued the tradition of the lighthouse as monumental structure. It was built on rocks that lie in the estuary of the River Gironde, obstructing passage from the Bay of Biscay into the busy wine-exporting port of Bordeaux. For most of the medieval period, this mortal hazard to shipping was marked by little more than a bonfire. Edward, the Black Prince, English ruler of the Bordeaux region, erected a tower upon the reef in *c.* 1360 and paid a hermit to maintain a fire at its summit. But the hermit died, the light often went unattended, and shipwrecks continued. In 1584, French architect and engineer Louis de Foix (*c.* 1535–1602) acquired a royal commission to build a new lighthouse on the reef. A man of grandiose vision, de Foix conceived a splendorous building that went far beyond the basic needs of a beacon for sailors. Elevated upon a stone platform that protected it from the pummeling waves, a fairy-tale Renaissance palace rose on the sea. Its lavishly decorated interior, rich in marble, carved wood, and mosaics, contained a splendid entrance hall, royal apartments – although no king ever set foot there – and a chapel with stained-glass windows. The wood-fired light on top of the tower seemed almost an afterthought. Exhausted and bankrupted by his labors, de Foix did not live to see the Cordouan tower completed in 1611. His work, although extended upward in more austere style by later hands, still stands today.

No such elaborate structures existed around the coasts of the British Isles. In 1566, during the reign of Queen Elizabeth I, the English parliament passed the Seamarks Act, which entrusted the Brethren of Trinity House of Deptford Strond with erecting "beacons, marks, and signs for the sea" so that ships might "better come into their ports without peril." Originally a mariners' association or guild, founded in 1514, Trinity House was to become world famous for its system of lighthouses, but its initial performance in this sphere was lamentable. There is no record of the Brethren having built a beacon for the next forty years, and even after that progress was patchy. Private enterprise rushed in to fill the vacuum. Any landowner with property on the coast might petition the monarch for the right to build a lighthouse, to be financed by charging dues on ships using the nearest port.

6.

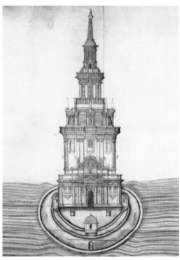

7.

Fig. 6.— *The primitive 14th-century Cordouan light in the Gironde estuary.*

Fig. 7.— *A palace on the sea: Louis de Foix's spectacular Cordouan lighthouse.*

Fig. 8.— *The light on Scotland's Isle of May was a coal-fueled brazier, the coal raised by a winch.*

Fig. 9.— *The foundations of the Smeaton lighthouse on the Eddystone reef.*

Fig. 10.— *Circular hole cut into the Bell Rock for the foundations of the lighthouse begun in 1807.*

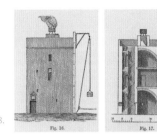

8.

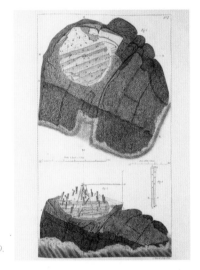

9.

10.

The inevitable consequence was a rash of poor-quality beacons around the shores of England and Wales, for which shipowners were required to pay excessive dues. Trinity House itself depended on private entrepreneurs to build lighthouses that it then acquired at a high price. This unsatisfactory situation was allowed to continue into the early 19th century.

Ireland and Scotland did not come within the remit of Trinity House. The first light tower in Ireland was built in the 13th century at Hook Head, east of Waterford harbor, the open fire on its roof tended by monks from a nearby monastery. Little further progress was made until the 1660s, when King Charles II authorized Sir Robert Reading (c. 1640-89), a member of the Irish parliament, to build a series of beacons at locations including Old Head of Kinsale in County Cork. This gave the Irish a clear lead over the Scots, for in the 17th century there existed only a single lighthouse in the whole of Scotland. This stood on the Isle of May, a rocky menace to shipping at the entrance to the Firth of Forth. There, in 1636, a plain squat tower was erected with a brazier on its roof. The laborers entrusted with tending the beacon raised coal to the top of the tower via a pulley. Burned in the brazier, the coal provided an amount of light and smoke that might, under ideal weather conditions, give at least some warning to sailors. However, high wind or poor visibility rendered it useless. The Isle of May lighthouse persisted in this primitive form for 180 years.

English engineer John Smeaton's success in taming the Eddystone Rock in southwest England in 1759 (see Prologue) marked the beginning of the golden age of lighthouse building. By that time, inspired by the practical rationalism of the European Enlightenment, determined efforts were being made to improve life through the application of science to practical inventions. The growth of trade and productivity was being encouraged not only as a source of wealth but also as the key to the progress of civilization. The development of the lighthouse took its place as part of this self-conscious march of progress, alongside the steam engine and the spinning jenny, the marine chronometer, and gas lighting. Over the following 150 years, lighthouses were built on cliffs, islands, rocks, and reefs around the world, from Japan to New Zealand, from the Baltic to the Red Sea, from the Arctic Circle to Tierra del Fuego.

As countries with overseas empires and rapidly expanding maritime trade, Britain and France naturally took the lead in lighthouse building. The urgent need for a reduction in the incidence of shipwreck was self-evident. It is reckoned that by the 1790s more than five hundred ships were being wrecked around the coasts of Britain every year. Yet not everyone wanted change. Many impoverished coastal communities depended for their survival upon the plundering of wrecked ships. Regarding shipwrecks as God's bounty to the poor, they were resolutely hostile to any measure that might improve maritime safety. More surprisingly, sailors often opposed the building of lighthouses, as they were skeptical of all novelties and accepted the heavy loss of life in their profession with fatalistic indifference. However, pressure from the mercantile interest – anyone who was liable to lose money when a ship went down – and from naval officers proved decisive. Safety of the seas was seen as necessary for national prosperity and naval power. The authorities were called upon to provide more and better lighthouses, and eventually they did.

The lamentable lack of lighthouses in Scotland was addressed through the establishment of the Commissioners of Northern Light Houses, later renamed the Northern Lighthouse Board, in 1786. In the same year, the Commissioners of Irish Lights were given responsibility for aids to navigation in Ireland. In France, the Service des Phares et Balises (Service of Lighthouses and Seamarks) was founded in 1806 as a subsection of the country's already well-established engineering bureaucracy. Trinity House very belatedly assumed full centralized control of the administration and construction of lighthouses in England and Wales in 1836. Meanwhile, civil engineering had emerged as a recognized profession, meeting the need for new roads and bridges, ports, and canals, as well as lighthouses. The world's first school of civil engineering, the École Nationale des Ponts et Chaussées, was created in France in 1747. In Britain, Eddystone builder Smeaton founded the Society of Civil Engineers (later known as the Smeatonian Society of Civil Engineers) in 1771. The new professionalism gradually made its mark in taller and sturdier lighthouse towers, and also in a heroic response to the challenge of building lighthouses on the most exposed reefs and rocks.

11.

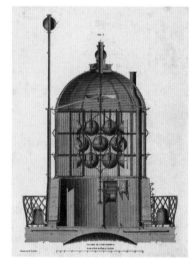

12.

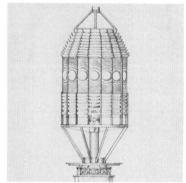

13.

Fig. 11.— *The lantern of Smeaton's Eddystone, weakly lit by candles.*

Fig. 12.— *The catoptric light system with Argand lamps and parabolic reflectors used in Stevenson's Bell Rock lighthouse (1810).*

Fig. 13.— *A Fresnel lens, the device that revolutionized lighthouses from the 1820s by generating a powerful beam.*

Fig. 14.— *Stages in the construction of Reynaud's Héaux de Bréhat lighthouse off the coast of Brittany.*

14.

Organizational improvements and the building skills of civil engineers would have been of no worth without radical advancements in lighting and optics. Simple tallow candles and wood- or coal-fueled fires were slowly supplanted by oil-burning Argand lamps, invented in 1780 by Aimé Argand (1750-1803). Already a major improvement, the effect of the oil lamps was augmented by the use of mirrors. The first parabolic mirror – in which the reflecting material covered the inner surface of a hollow half-sphere – was installed by Jonas Norberg (1711-83) at the Korsö lighthouse in Sweden in 1757. The pace of progress should not be exaggerated, though. According to one calculation, out of 254 lighthouses in Europe in 1819, only sixty used state-of-the-art Argand lamps and thirty-five still relied on wood or coal fires or candles. Nor was a combination of Argand lamps and mirrors necessarily fully adequate. It was not until the adoption of the Fresnel lens, after its successful trial in 1823, that a truly effective beam could be generated (see Chapter 3).

The French, with their admirable respect for reason, followed a systematic plan to create a continuous chain of lighthouses along their coast, so that sailors would always have at least one light in their field of view. Most of these were land lights, sited on mainland cliffs or substantial islands, but along the wave-tormented coast of Brittany, French engineers had to cope with the challenge of building on outlying reefs that were all but inaccessible. The achievement of engineer Léonce Reynaud (1803-80) in creating the Héaux de Bréhat tower off the north Breton coast in 1840 was an epic feat of skill and perseverance.

The British proceeded with less logic than the French, in a manner that could sometimes seem amateurish. Take, for example, the story of the Smalls lighthouse. A dangerous collection of rocks off St. David's Head, Pembrokeshire, the Smalls was private property in the 18th century. In 1773, the landowner decided to build a lighthouse on the rocks, choosing as his engineer a young craftsman, Henry Whiteside, who made violins and harpsichords for a living. Whiteside created an ungainly skeletal wooden structure, with oak piles supporting living quarters and a lantern that emitted a feeble light. Described contemptuously by the great Scottish engineer Robert Stevenson (1772-1850) as "a raft of timber rudely put together," this structure remarkably survived decades of battering by winter storms.

Even after Trinity House took over responsibility for the Smalls in 1836, the archaic wooden lighthouse was allowed to remain in operation until tardily and reluctantly replaced with a state-of-the-art stone tower in 1861. Nevertheless, if in no very logical manner, the coasts of England and Wales were lit over the course of the 19th century, most notably through the efforts of chief engineer James Walker (1781-1862). His achievements - ranging from the picturesque land light at Start Point, south Devon, completed in 1836, to the spectacular Atlantic lighthouse of Bishop Rock (1858) off the Isles of Scilly - were among the most challenging projects of the entire era. The English also pioneered the screw-pile lighthouse, an iron structure suitable for erection on sand or mudflats, the first examples of which were built at Maplin Sands in the Thames Estuary and off Fleetwood, Lancashire, in *c.* 1840.

Some of the most notable feats of lighthouse building in the 19th century were achieved in Scotland under the aegis of the Northern Lighthouse Board. Its first chief engineer was Thomas Smith (1752-1814), a lamp maker who had made his reputation providing Edinburgh with street lighting. After building four lighthouses, including North Ronaldsay (1789) in the Orkneys and the Mull of Kintyre (1788), Smith passed on the job to his young stepson Robert Stevenson. A national hero after the successful completion of a lighthouse on Bell Rock in 1810, Stevenson founded a remarkable family dynasty of lighthouse engineers who served the Northern Lighthouse Board through to World War II.

Three of Stevenson's four sons were prolific lighthouse builders. David (1815-86) and Thomas (1818-87) Stevenson, the two younger sons, worked together on some thirty lighthouses, including the most northerly lighthouse in Britain on Muckle Flugga in Shetland (originally named North Unst, now known as Muckle Flugga lighthouse) completed in 1858. But it was the second son, Alan (1807-65), who probably deserves the highest reputation, both for his achievement in building the lofty rock lighthouse at Skerryvore in 1844 and for his ingenious improvements to lighthouse optics. The black sheep of the family was Thomas's son, Robert Louis Stevenson, who uniquely resisted the pressure to follow in his father's and grandfather's footsteps, becoming a writer instead of an engineer and ending up more famous than any of his

THE LIGHTHOUSE IS THE GREATEST BLESSING THAT HAS BEEN BESTOWED UPON NAVIGATION.

FREDERICK A. TALBOT
1913

Fig. 15.— Whiteside's ungainly wooden Smalls lighthouse off the coast of Wales.

Fig. 16.— The 1716 Boston light, the first lighthouse built in the United States.

Fig. 17.— Sandy Hook light (1764) in New Jersey, the oldest extant lighthouse in the United States.

15.

16.

17.

relatives. By the end of the 19th century, the Stevenson family had endowed Scotland with what is sometimes claimed to be the world's most impressive array of lighthouses.

The United States was not initially a world leader in lighthouse construction. Still, its lighthouse tradition started quite well in the colonial era. Massachusetts claims the honor of having built the first lighthouse in the future United States in 1716. The Boston light, sited on Little Brewster Island, was a tower some 70 feet (21 m) tall, initially mounting a lantern with tallow candles - a seriously underpowered light source. The original tower was destroyed in the American War of Independence, first burned by the Americans and then blown up by the British. Rebuilt in 1783, it still stands today. However, New Jersey's Sandy Hook light, a finely executed stone octagon at the southern entrance to New York harbor, has stood intact since 1764 and so takes the accolade for the oldest working lighthouse in the United States. It is not the oldest in North America, though. The still-functioning Sambro Island lighthouse at the mouth of Halifax harbor in Nova Scotia, Canada, predates the Sandy Hook light by five years.

After independence, President George Washington signed a law giving the federal government responsibility for all US lighthouses in 1789. The first federal lighthouse was completed in 1791 at Portland Head in Maine. Others followed, most famously the stone tower at Montauk Point on Long Island, New York, in 1796, especially associated with Washington because as a young man he had allegedly identified the site as suitable for a lighthouse back in the 1750s. Heading into the 1800s, however, the impetus of US lighthouse building sadly declined. Under the tight-fisted leadership of Treasury Department official Stephen Pleasonton for three decades from 1820, the US Lighthouse Service achieved an expansion in the number of lighthouses, from around seventy to more than three hundred, but quality did not match quantity. Many were simply ordinary houses of one or two stories, with a lantern on the roof. Where towers were built, they were often of poor quality and were soon tottering and crumbling. Worse than the cheapness of the buildings was the inadequacy of the lights. Pleasonton adopted a system of illumination proposed by a former sea captain, Winslow Lewis, which used an Argand oil lamp in association with a mirror and a convex lens. It was extremely inexpensive and desperately ineffectual. Only a very few of the state-of-the-art Fresnel lenses then being introduced in Europe found their way across the Atlantic.

The inertia of the Pleasonton era was ended by a disaster, which ironically resulted from over-bold innovation. Minot's Ledge, southeast of Boston Harbor, was a notorious hazard to shipping. In 1847, work began on an iron-pile lighthouse design derived from those recently pioneered in England. With its keepers' dwelling and lantern on a platform supported by iron legs drilled into the submerged rock, this skeletal structure was successfully completed in 1850. Public attention had been drawn to Minot's Ledge by a tragic shipwreck that occurred when construction was under way: the wreck of a vessel carrying Irish immigrants fleeing Ireland's Great Famine in October 1849, which resulted in more than one hundred deaths. Much was riding on the lighthouse's success. But on April 17, 1851, a storm swept the Massachusetts coast and carried away the newly built Minot's Ledge light along with its two keepers. Responding to a public outcry at the inadequate state of the nation's lighthouses, Congress appointed a new Lighthouse Board under Admiral William Shubrick and gave him the money to do the job properly.

Under this new regime, Fresnel lenses were bought in from Europe to equip a fresh generation of lighthouses that transformed US coastal navigation. US Army engineers such as George Meade (1815-72) - later the victorious commander at the Battle of Gettysburg (1863) in the Civil War - were used to bring a new professionalism to lighthouse building. The lost light at Minot's Ledge was replaced by an English-style granite tower, although many of the new lighthouses built in the 1850s followed the skeletal iron design that had failed so spectacularly at Minot's Ledge. Some of Meade's screw-pile iron lighthouses - for example, those at Sand Key (1853) and Sombrero Key (1858) in hurricane-plagued Florida - still stand today. A civilian engineer, Francis Gibbons, was commissioned to build the first lighthouses on the United States' Pacific coast, beginning at Alcatraz Island in San Francisco Bay in 1853. The Civil War that tore the United States apart from 1861 to 1865 necessarily had a deleterious effect on the nation's lighthouses, but after its end the march of progress resumed. With Colonel Orlando Metcalfe Poe (1832-95) as chief

IRON LIGHT HOUSE, ON MINOT'S LEDGE, OFF COHASSET, MASS. BAY.

18.

19.

Fig. 18.— The iron skeleton lighthouse at Minot's Ledge off Massachusetts, a bold but fatally flawed design.

Fig. 19.— The iron Minot's Ledge light collapsed in the heavy seas of April 17, 1851.

Fig. 20.— Stannard Rock lighthouse in Lake Superior, a triumph of US engineering in the 1880s.

Fig. 21.— Built in France, the cast-iron Amédée lighthouse was shipped to New Caledonia in the South Pacific.

engineer to the Lighthouse Board, a string of remarkable lighthouses was built on the Great Lakes, including Spectacle Reef Light on Lake Huron (1874) and Stannard Rock Light on Lake Superior (1883). These were built on a caisson or crib, which created a solid concrete foundation for the light towers, capable of resisting the formidable pressure of the lakes' winter ice.

The geographical spread of lighthouses through the second half of the 19th century advanced in step with the growth of European imperialism, the rapid rise in global maritime trade, and the introduction of ocean-going steamships. To profit from their worldwide commercial and military dominance, the European powers needed to make distant waters as safe as their own. Japan, for example, forcibly opened to foreign trade from 1854, was more or less ordered by the Western powers to establish modern lighthouses. Sent to Japan by the Scottish Stevensons' firm in 1868, engineer Richard Brunton (1841–1901) served the imperial government for eight years, during which time he supervised the building of twenty-six Western-style lighthouses. Having acquired the necessary expertise, Japanese engineers then took over the continued expansion of their own lighthouse system. To give another example, in the 1850s the British government was so concerned about the inadequacy of the existing navigational aids in Canada that it paid for the construction of a series of tall "imperial" lighthouses on the Great Lakes and the Atlantic coast.

For the construction of lighthouses in some of the more undeveloped areas of their colonial empires, British and French engineers turned to prefabricated iron structures. The first of these in the British Empire was the Morant Point lighthouse in Jamaica in 1841. Buildings of this type were constructed in the home country out of cast-iron components. They were then disassembled and the parts shipped in crates to their distant destination, where they were erected for a second time using local labor. The first lighthouse in New Zealand, established at Pencarrow Head in 1859, was another cast-iron structure shipped across the world from England. The French followed suit with the lofty Amédée lighthouse installed in New Caledonia in the South Pacific in 1865. They were so delighted with the Amédée light that they employed the same technique to erect a lighthouse on the reef at Roches-Douvres near Guernsey in 1868. Before

20.

21.

being transported to its permanent site, the Roches-Douvres lighthouse stood on the Champ de Mars in Paris as one of the exhibits for the Universal Exposition of 1867.

Initially, Germany had not been at the forefront of lighthouse development, but from the mid-19th century it quickly made up for lost time. The Bremerhaven lighthouse in the North Sea port, built between 1853 and 1855, showed the Germans' new ambition. A brick tower, designed by Bremen architect Simon Loschen (1818–1902) in the Gothic style, it was a striking contribution to the monumental tradition of lighthouse building. After the unification of Germany in 1871, estuaries, coasts, ports, and offshore islands were peppered with new lighthouses. The most striking examples included the Borkum Grosser light (1879), on Borkum Island in Lower Saxony, one of the world's tallest brick-built lighthouses at 197 feet (60 m), and the fine cast-iron 130-foot (40-m) Westerheversand tower built in Schleswig-Holstein in 1908.

22.

One of Germany's major lighthouse builders was the Helios electrical company, based in the Ehrenfeld suburb of Cologne. A lighthouse they erected at their Ehrenfeld plant, once used as a test facility, still flashes its beam across Cologne's night sky today.

23.

The scale of lighthouse building worldwide in the late 19th and early 20th centuries was phenomenal. For example, Australia, then a country with a population of less than five million people, had 103 manned lights by 1915. Scottish engineer George Slight (1859–1934), employed as head of the Chilean lighthouse service in 1893, built some seventy lighthouses in two decades. William Anderson (1851–1927), superintendent of lighthouses in Canada for forty years from 1880, is said to have supervised the installation of more than five hundred Canadian lights. In addition, the building of US lighthouses continued apace, including the first ten lighthouses in Alaska built between 1902 and 1906. In 1905, the Norwegians built the northernmost lighthouse on the European mainland: the cast-iron Slettnes lighthouse, standing at a latitude of 71 degrees north, deep within the Arctic Circle. Furthermore, technical advancements abounded, from the use of steel and ferroconcrete as building materials to innovations in lighting, including the use first of kerosene and then, increasingly, of acetylene and electric power. The entire global system was maintained by the

24.

Fig. 22.— The 1868 cast-iron Roches-Douvres lighthouse near Guernsey.

Fig. 23.— The Gothic-style light at the German port of Bremen, built in the 1850s.

Fig. 24.— The cast-iron tower of Westerheversand light in northern Germany.

Fig. 25.— The lighthouse built at Borkum in the East Friesian Islands in 1879.

Fig. 26.— The German Heligoland light of 1902 with its powerful electric beam.

meticulously inspected and supervised work of teams of lighthouse keepers, operating to internationally accepted rules and standards.

It is impossible to establish a precise date for the end of a phenomenon as inherently vague as "the golden age of lighthouses," but certainly by the 1920s the lights' technological preeminence and symbolic mystique had passed their zenith. The invention of aircraft opened up a new heroic frontier, where human courage and technical ingenuity pitted themselves against the elements. Skyscrapers dwarfed lighthouses as feats of architecture. Radios and radio beacons came into use, reducing the central importance of the light itself. As automatic control systems spread, increasing numbers of lights were able to dispense with the lonely vigil of their lighthouse keepers.

On the one hand, lighthouses had become an integrated practical element in a mature functioning system of global maritime navigation. On the other, they were developing a retro charm, as an established part of the iconography of beach vacations featured on postcards and railroad advertisements, or welcome landmarks for healthy hikers. Long before the worldwide system of lights entered into its late 20th-century decline, lighthouses had become relics of the past rather than symbols of the future, proud memorials of distant feats of engineering, largely forgotten acts of personal heroism, and a lost way of life.

25.

26.

00 TOWER OF HERCULES
GALICIA | SPAIN

ORIGINALLY DESIGNED BY GAIUS SEVIUS LUPUS
TOWER: **SQUARE BRICK WITH STONE FACING**
HEIGHT: **111 FT (34 M)** | LIGHT: **FIRE IN BRAZIER**

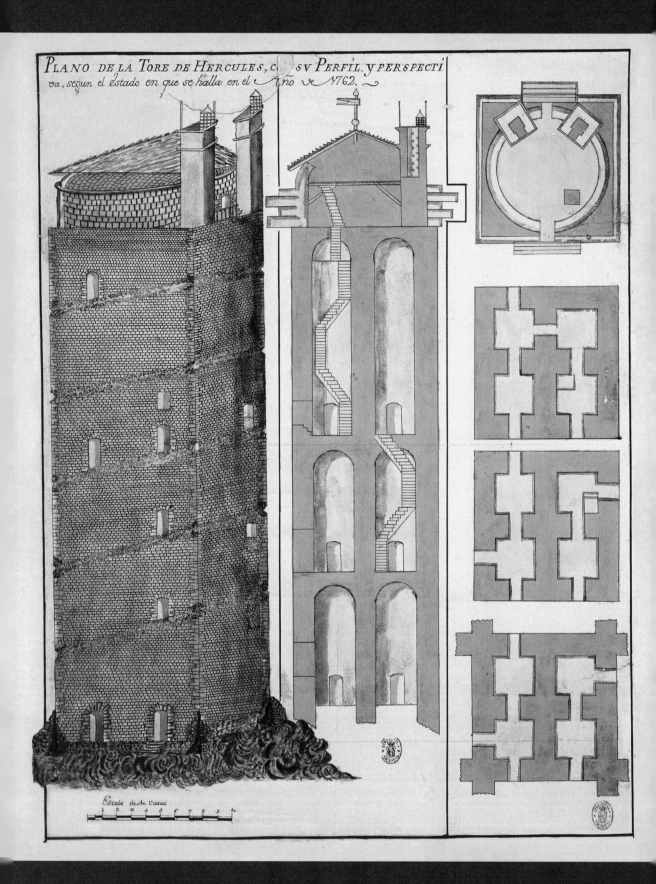

Plano de la Tore de Hercules, con su Perfil, y perspectiva, segun el estado en que se halla en el Año de 1762.

Escala de 50 Varas
1 2 3 4 5 6 7 8 9

Probably built in the reign of the Roman emperor Trajan, the Tower of Hercules guided ships to the Roman port of Brigantium, now A Coruña. The original three-story building was faced with stone and had a spiral ramp running around the outside, giving access to a domed lantern. By the time

the above drawings were made in 1762, the ramp had long disappeared and an internal wooden staircase had been added in the 17th century. In 1790, the lighthouse was rebuilt as a four-story tower (bottom right and far right). This still stands today, the world's oldest functioning lighthouse.

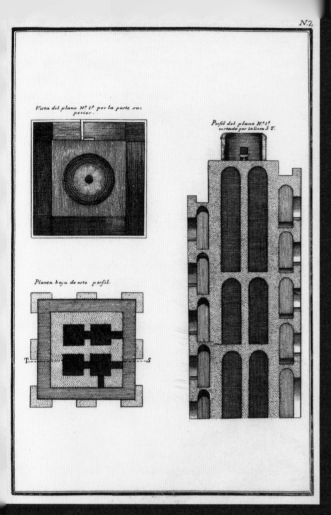

Vista del plano N.º 1.º por la parte superior.

Perfil del plano N.º 1.º cortado por la línea S T.

Planta baja de este perfil.

T — S

Escala de 30 varas castellanas.

Escala de 30 varas castellanas.

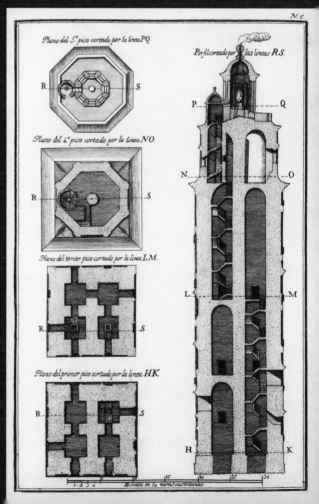

Plano del 5.º piso cortado por la línea P Q.

R — S

Plano del 4.º piso cortado por la línea N O.

R — S

Plano del tercer piso cortado por la línea L M.

R — S

Plano del primer piso cortado por la línea H K.

R — S

Perfil cortado por las líneas R S.

P — Q

N — O

L — M

H — K

Escala de 30 varas castellanas.

Elevation de la Tour prise par la
ligne   A · B.

Coupe de la Tour prise par la
ligne   C.D.

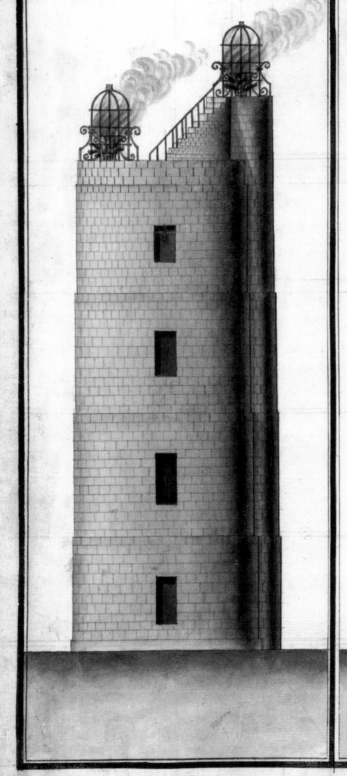

Echelle de dix Toises communes

The first Chassiron lighthouse was built at the northwestern extremity of Oléron island on the orders of King Louis XIV's finance minister, Colbert. The tower overlooked the Antioch narrows, a notorious site of shipwrecks on the approaches to the port of Rochefort. A double light was installed to differentiate Chassiron from other French west coast lighthouses at Cordouan and on the Île de Ré. A pulley was used to lift wood up the tower to fuel the braziers in the lanterns. The tower served for 150 years until it was replaced by the current lighthouse at Chassiron in 1836.

Autre Coupe de la même Tour prise par la ligne E F.

PLANS PROFILS COUPE
ET ELEVATION DE LA TOUR
CHASSIRON
scituée a la pointe du bout du monde en L'I
D'OLLERON en l'etat que cette tour e
en 1716
elle est destinée a servir de Fanal pour eclairer au
vaisseaux. qui viennent de la mer, ou on alume, tou
les soirs. deux feux de bois dans des cages ou rechaux
pour les distinguer de celuy des tours des balaines et de Cord

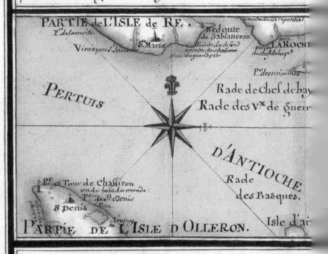

Echelle de 3 lieues commune de France pour la Car

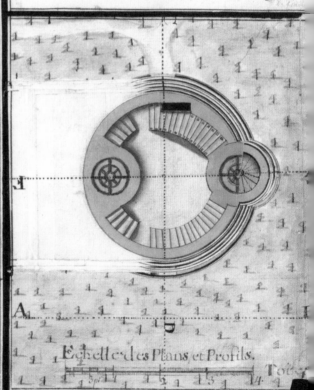

Echelle des Plans et Profils.

Coupes Profils et Elevations

1691 NORTH FORELAND
KENT | ENGLAND

DESIGNER **UNKNOWN** | TOWER: **OCTAGONAL**
STONE AND FLINT | ORIGINAL HEIGHT: **85 FT**
(26 M) | ORIGINAL LIGHT: **COAL FIRE**

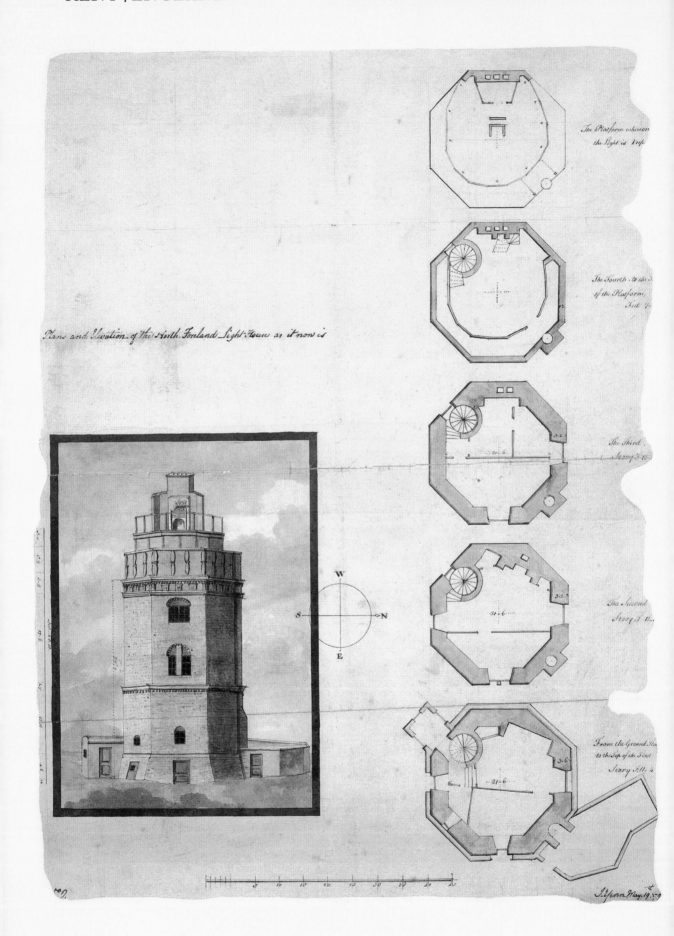

The cliffs of the North Foreland command the Goodwin Sands, a hazard to shipping entering the Thames Estuary. The 1691 tower replaced an earlier wooden lighthouse destroyed in 1683. Its open fire reportedly burned 100 tons of coal a year. An attempt to enclose the fire in the 1730s was abandoned after mariners complained that it made the light less visible. Around 1793 the lighthouse was raised by two stories to a height of 100 ft (30 m) and the fire was replaced by Argand lamps and parabolic reflectors. North Foreland was the last English lighthouse to be automated, in 1998.

1733 **LOUISBOURG**
NOVA SCOTIA | CANADA

DESIGNED BY **ÉTIENNE VERRIER** | TOWER:
CIRCULAR STONE WITH WOOD AND GLASS
LANTERN | HEIGHT: **65 FT (20 M)** | LIGHT: **FIRE**

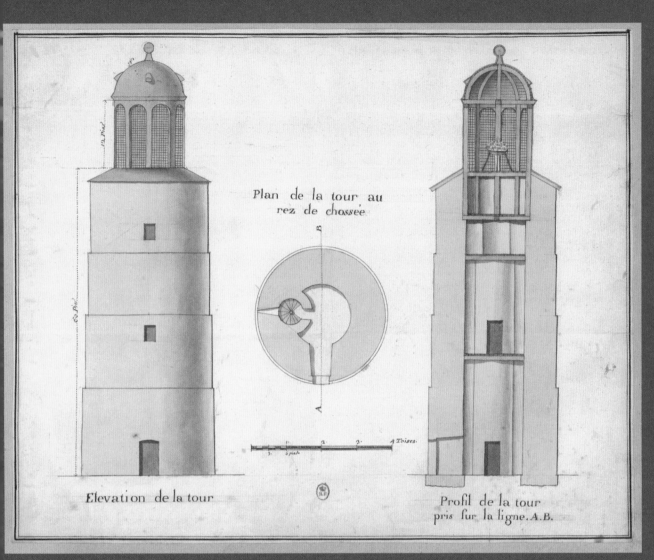

Plan de la tour au
rez de chossée

Elevation de la tour

Profil de la tour
pris fur la ligne. A.B.

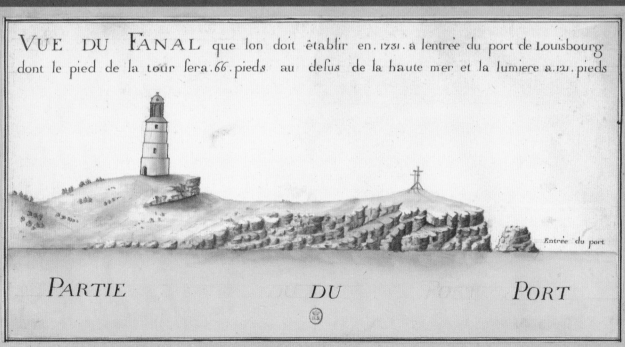

VUE DU FANAL que lon doit établir en. 1731. à lentrée du port de Louisbourg
dont le pied de la tour fera. 66. pieds au defus de la haute mer et la lumiere a. 121. pieds

PARTIE   DU   PORT

Entrée du port

In the 1730s Louisbourg on Cape Breton Island was a French
colonial port and fortress. The lighthouse copied the design
of the Phare des Baleines on the Île de Ré in western France.
In 1758, the British besieged and captured Louisbourg;
damaged in the fighting, the lighthouse was abandoned.

1757 **KORSÖ**
KORSÖ ISLAND | SWEDEN

LIGHT DESIGNED BY **JONAS NORBERG**
TOWER: **CIRCULAR STONE** | HEIGHT: **75FT (23 M)**
LIGHT: **CANDLES WITH PARABOLIC MIRRORS**

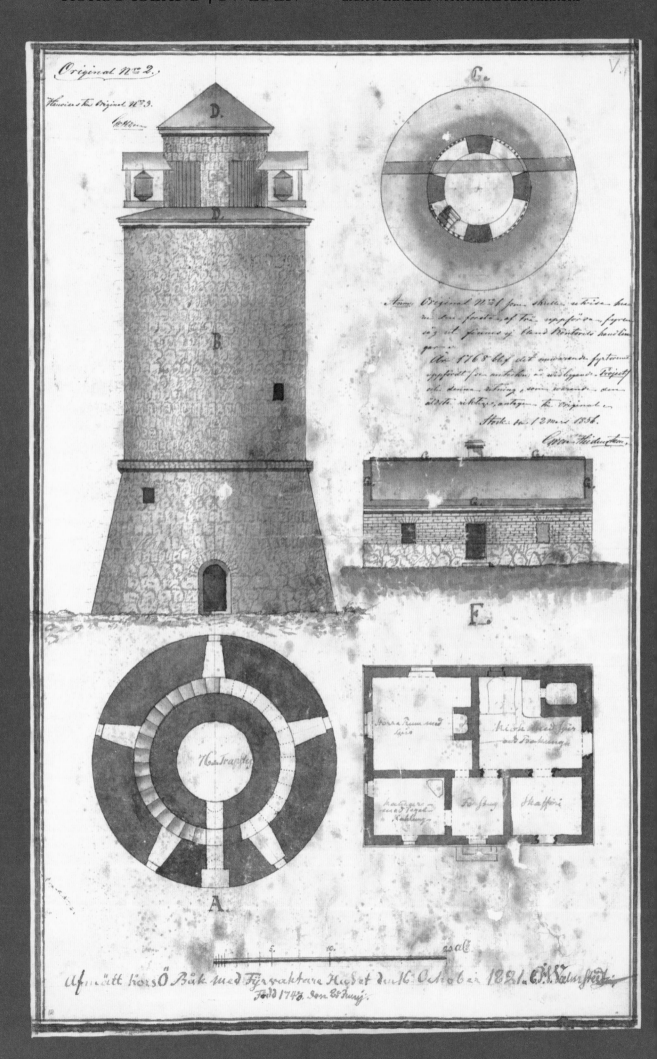

OPPOSITE The lighthouse on Korsö island in the Stockholm Archipelago was notable for Jonas Norberg's innovative use of parabolic mirrors to enhance the light. He also created the first flashing light by rotating the mirrors with a clockwork mechanism. The lighthouse has been inactive since 1882.

ABOVE This light formed part of a Swedish military fortress built with convict labor. It boasted the world's first revolving light, the creation of Jonas Norberg. Driven by clockwork, the light installation completed a revolution every five minutes. The fortress lighthouse ceased functioning in 1868.

Elevation d'un Phare à construire à l'isle de Batz, sud la Pointte de Chuch Chidis.

Vû par Nous, Ingénieur en Chef du Dépt. du Finistère, à quimper le 1er Pluviose, l'an b. David.

n°. 6.

1811 **BELL ROCK**
ARBROATH | SCOTLAND

DESIGNED BY **ROBERT STEVENSON** | TOWER:
CIRCULAR STONE | HEIGHT: **116 FT (35 M)**
LIGHT: **OIL LAMPS WITH REFLECTORS**

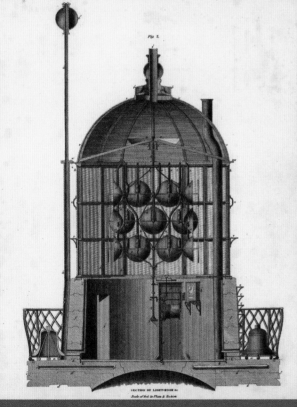

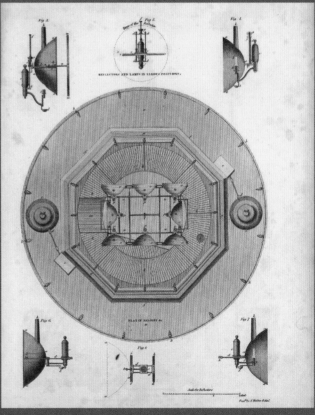

OPPOSITE This ambitious plan for a lighthouse on the Île de Batz off the coast of Brittany was drawn up by the Naval Ministry in Year IV of the revolutionary calendar, 1795–96, but the tower was never built. A lighthouse was finally constructed on the Île de Batz forty years later, in 1836.

ABOVE Standing on the Bell Rock reef off the east coast of Scotland, the lighthouse was built between 1807 and 1810. Robert Stevenson, as chief engineer of the Northern Lighthouse Board, designed a tapering granite tower topped by a lantern with Argand lamps and twenty-four parabolic reflectors.

1824 **GREEN POINT | CAPE TOWN | S. AFRICA**

DESIGNED BY **HERMANN SCHÜTTE** | TOWER: **SQUARE STONE WITH TWO LANTERNS** | HEIGHT: **52 FT (16 M)** | LIGHT: **ARGAND OIL LAMPS**

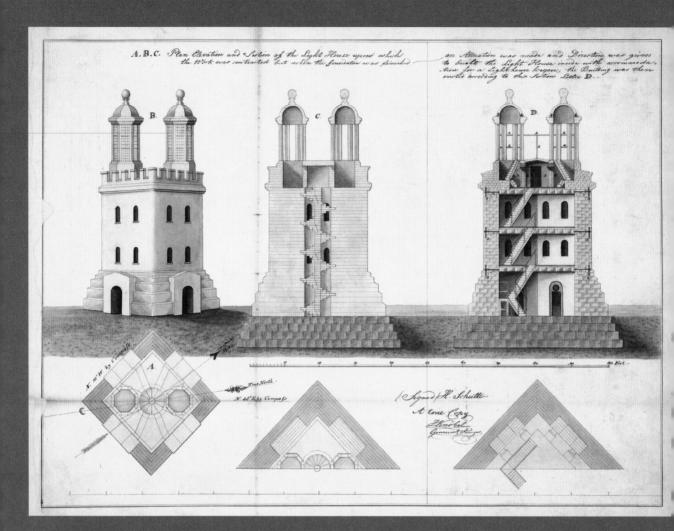

1826 LONGSTONE
NORTHUMBERLAND | ENGLAND

DESIGNED BY **JOSEPH NELSON** | TOWER:
CIRCULAR STONE | HEIGHT: **85 FT (26 M)** | ORIGINAL
LIGHT: **ARGAND OIL LAMPS AND REFLECTORS**

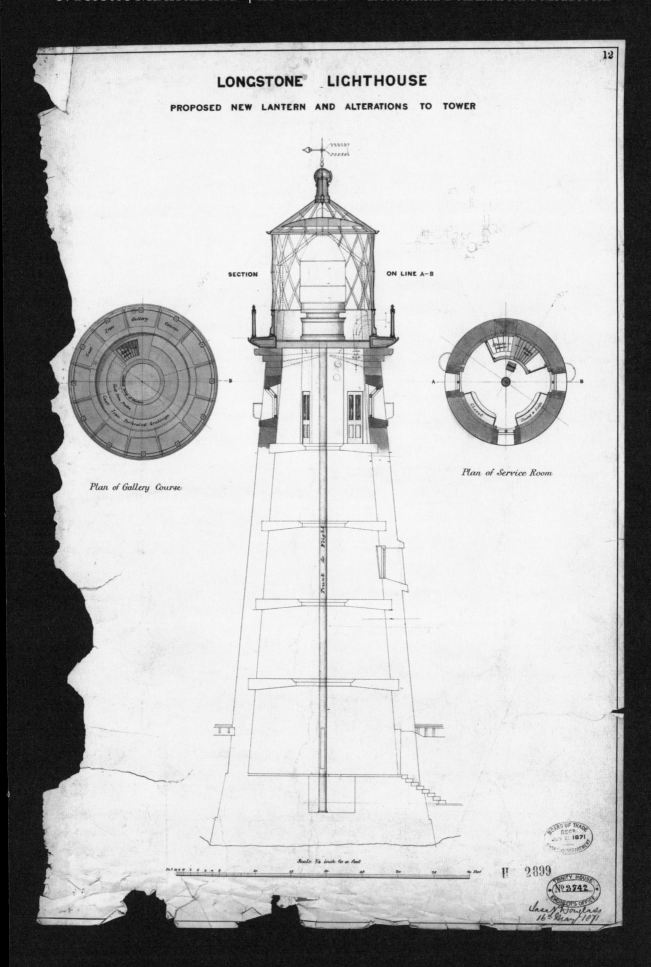

LONGSTONE LIGHTHOUSE

PROPOSED NEW LANTERN AND ALTERATIONS TO TOWER

12

SECTION   ON LINE A–B

Plan of Gallery Course

Plan of Service Room

Scale ½ inch to a foot

H 2899

OPPOSITE Green Point lighthouse, designed by stonecutter Hermann Schütte, was the first lighthouse built in South Africa. Its role was to guide ships into Cape Town's Table Bay. The lighthouse was rebuilt in 1865 with a single lantern, essentially to the shape it has today.

ABOVE Famous as the Grace Darling lighthouse, the Longstone light stands in the Farne Islands off England's northeastern coast. This plan shows proposed alterations to the original light carried out in the 1870s, chiefly the installation of a Fresnel lens made by the Birmingham firm Chance Brothers.

1827 CAPE ARKONA
RÜGEN | GERMANY

DESIGNED BY **KARL FRIEDRICH SCHINKEL**
TOWER: **SQUARE BRICK** | HEIGHT: **63 FT (19 M)**
ORIGINAL LIGHT: **OIL BURNERS AND REFLECTORS**

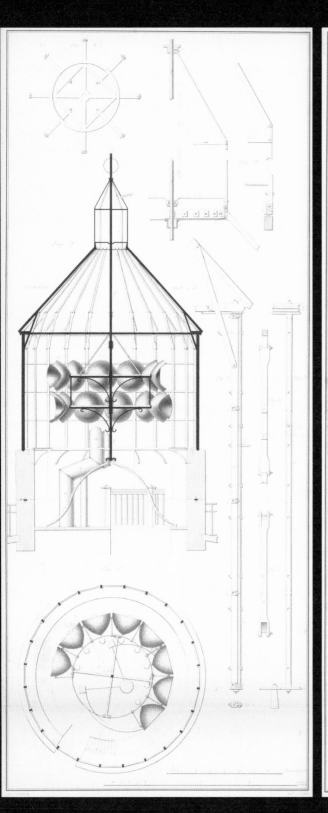

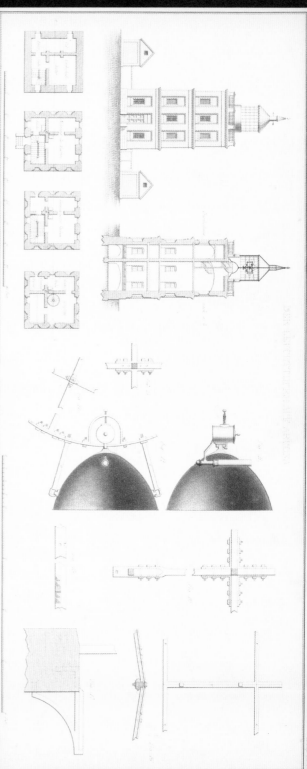

At the north end of Rügen island in the Baltic, the first Cape Arkona lighthouse was built by the Prussian state between 1826 and 1827. Its light consisted of seventeen parabolic reflectors and lamps burning rapeseed oil, later converted to kerosene. A new light was built alongside the old in 1902-05.

1830 GREENORE COUNTY LOUTH | IRELAND

DESIGNED BY **GEORGE HALPIN** | TOWER: **CIRCULAR STONE** | HEIGHT: **36 FT (11 M)** LIGHT: **OIL LAMPS AND REFLECTORS**

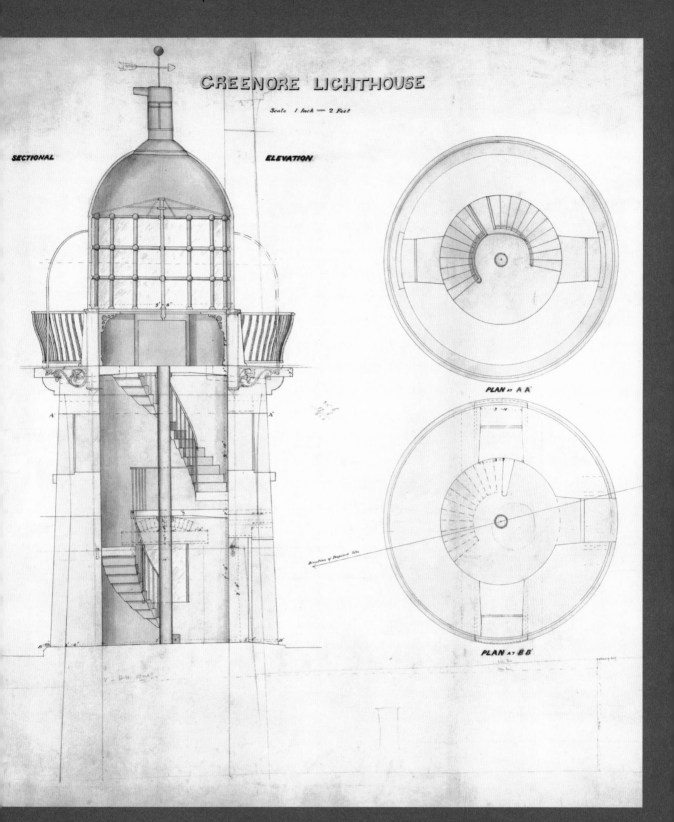

GREENORE LICHTHOUSE

Scale 1 Inch = 2 Feet

SECTIONAL

ELEVATION

PLAN AT A A'

PLAN AT B B'

This lighthouse at the entrance to Carlingford Lough, now part of the border between the Republic of Ireland and Northern Ireland, was built by the Commissioners of Irish Lights. Their engineer George Halpin is credited with creating more than fifty new lighthouses. Greenore light has been out of service since 1986.

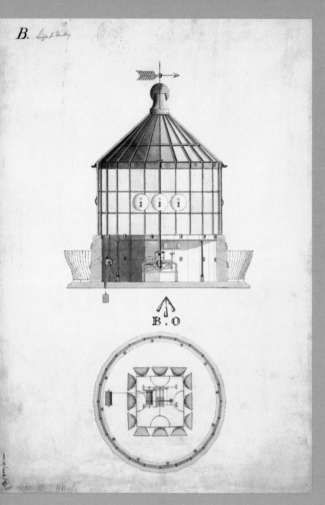

B.

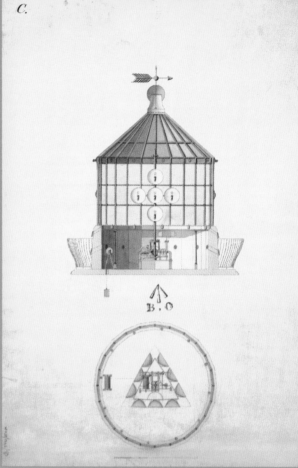

C.

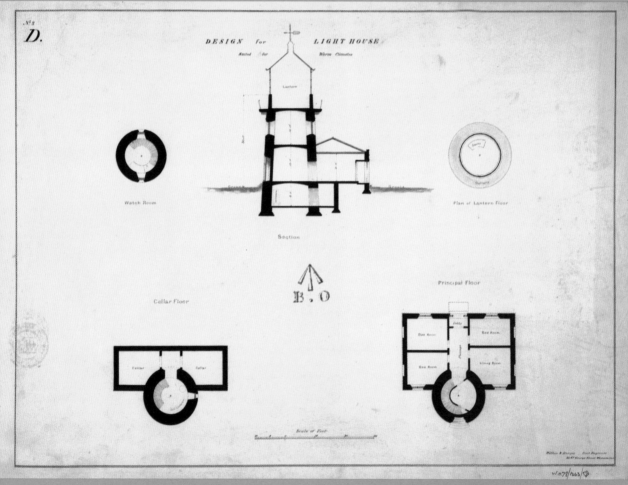

D.

DESIGN for LIGHT HOUSE

Suited for Warm Climates

Lantern

Watch Room

Plan of Lantern Floor

Section

Cellar Floor

Principal Floor

Scale of Feet

In 1833, Trinity House chief engineer James Walker's engineering consultancy firm, Walker & Burges, drew up generic plans for lighthouses to be built in "warm climates." The British were under pressure from the US government to build lighthouses in the Bahamas, where much US shipping was being lost to shipwreck. The drawings show different arrangements of oil lamps with parabolic reflectors, as well as an elevation and ground plan for a tower with keeper's accommodation and a cellar. The specific suitability of these designs for "warm climates" is unclear, although a cellar might have provided cool storage.

CHAPTER 2.

DEFYING

THE ELEMENTS.

THE PERILOUS BUSINESS

OF LIGHTHOUSE BUILDING.

1.

OPPOSITE

Top left: A worker maneuvers a stone block during the construction of Stevenson's Bell Rock lighthouse, c. 1808.

Top right: Elevation of the Bell Rock tower showing the interior sections.

Center: A front view of the sheer crane used to lift blocks of prepared stone from a moored flat-bottomed boat to Bell Rock.

Center right: Bassey, the only horse used in the construction of Bell Rock, harnessed to the Woolwich Sling Cart used to transport stone.

Bottom left (top): John Rennie's design for Bell Rock.

Bottom left (center): Two workers man the sheer crane, winching stone from a flat-bottomed boat onto Bell Rock.

Bottom left (bottom): A worker supports and balances a stone block as it is hauled up onto the rock by the sheer crane.

Bottom right: Stevenson's designs for Bell Rock, showing proposals for the structure.

ABOVE

Fig. 1.— Lighthouse construction in the early 19th century at Bell Rock, Scotland.

Lighthouses have always been romantic. Lovers of the world's wild places have never objected to the presence of these lonely sentinels on remote cliffs or in secluded bays. Rather than impressing the stamp of humanity's dominance on nature, lighthouses evoke human frailty and isolation in the face of the elemental strength of the ocean and the winds. This image of a courageous presence asserted in the teeth of adversity explains the enduring attraction of stories of the building of rock lighthouses. The construction of these edifices - offshore on islets or reefs swept by oceanic waves - was an uneven struggle in which the human will engaged with forces far beyond its power to control and, by a near miracle of endurance and persistence, ultimately prevailed.

The building of a rock lighthouse was often triggered by a maritime disaster, some shipwreck so awful in its material or human loss that the authorities would be goaded into exploring the possibility of installing a light in an apparently impossible location exposed to the extremes of wind and wave. Bell Rock off east Scotland had long been known as a mortal hazard to shipping before the British warship HMS *York* struck the reef in January 1804 and sank with the loss of all 491 crew on board. Described by engineer Robert Stevenson (1772-1850) as a "fatal catastrophe of which history affords few examples," this shipwreck loosened public purse strings, thereby providing Stevenson with the funds to proceed with building the renowned Bell Rock light (1811). Almost a century later, the death of 242 crew and passengers in the wreck of the steamship *Drummond Castle* off Ushant, northwest France, in June 1896 motivated the building of the La Jument light (1911). One of France's great lighthouses, La Jument took seven years to build on a rock 980 feet (300 m) off shore.

The site of a rock lighthouse was likely to be submerged, except at low tide, and inaccessible in poor weather, which was much of the time in summer and almost all the time in winter. Consequently, the engineer's first necessary move was to make a survey of the reef in person, so that he (an engineer was always "he" in the 19th century) could identify a suitable location for the structure and establish the precise character of the surface upon which the building was to be constructed. But for that he needed to land on the rock or islet, and get off again. There, the whole enterprise might stall before it had properly started. Landing from a cutter or surf boat on a wave-washed rock was no easy task, and the right combination of weather and tide might offer only a vanishingly small window of opportunity for even the most cursory review. There is no doubt that an engineer carrying out an initial survey was risking his life. Take the case of Wolf Rock, chosen as the site for a lighthouse off southwest England, between Land's End and the Isles of Scilly. It was above water for only a few hours of the day. In July 1861, British engineer James Douglass (1826–98) succeeded with great difficulty in scrambling onto the rock, but when he had completed a brief survey the treacherous waters made it impossible for his boat to approach to take him off. Fortunately, he had brought a lifeline with him. As the rising tide threatened to cover the reef, Douglass dove into the icy swirling waters and was hauled, soaked but safe, into the boat.

Tillamook Rock, off the coast of Oregon, posed similar problems with a tragic outcome. The US Lighthouse Board set out to place a light in this exposed location in 1879, but the US engineer in charge at first found it impossible to land there. After many days waiting for ideal conditions, he finally succeeded in leaping ashore, but prudence obliged him to jump back into the boat after only a brief stay as a mounting swell threatened to leave him marooned. An experienced British engineer, John Trewavas, was then called in to carry out a more thorough survey. As he leapt from a surf boat onto the rock, Trewavas lost his footing and was promptly swept to his death by a Pacific roller.

In drawing up plans for a rock lighthouse, a 19th-century engineer could only make guesses about the most essential element in his calculations: the strength of the ocean at its moments of greatest fury. As Alan Stevenson (1807–65) wrote in 1850: "No systematic or intelligible attempt has been made practically to measure the force of the waves," which left the engineer to base his decisions about lighthouse structure on experience and instinct, "an extensive knowledge of what the sea has done against man, and how, and to what extent, man has succeeded in controlling the sea." The plans drafted to guide the construction work breathe a purity and rationality that belies the essential chanciness of the whole operation.

Starting work on the foundations of a rock lighthouse posed a truly formidable challenge. Early 19th-century engineers confronted this task with quite primitive tools

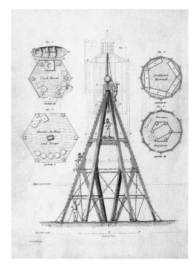

2.

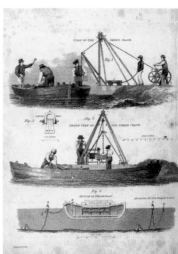

3.

Fig. 2.— *Building the beacon that eventually housed the workers at Bell Rock.*

Fig. 3.— *A crane unloads stone blocks brought by rowboat to Bell Rock.*

Fig. 4.— *The balance crane used to raise the stone blocks up the tower.*

Fig. 5.— *A rope bridge links the growing tower to the workers' barracks.*

Fig. 6.— *The Bell Rock tower is almost ready for the lantern to be fitted.*

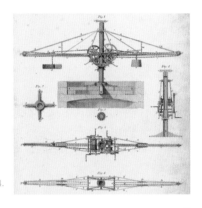

4.

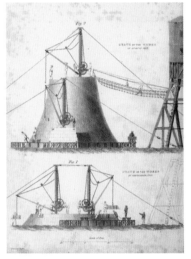

5.

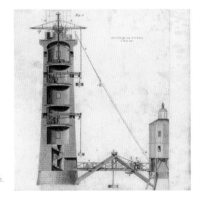

6.

at their disposal – picks and hammers to attack stone, horses to pull weights, sail and rowboats for transportation. As the century progressed, technological innovations such as steam boats and dynamite to level the rock rendered building work far easier, but nothing could make the battering of the elements less extreme. While an area of the rock was being leveled and the base of a tower set upon it, workers had no protection. They had to be ferried to and fro through dangerous restless waters and, if they were able to land, could only stay for the duration of low tide. In 1867, for example, the French took the bold decision to build a lighthouse on Ar-Men Rock off the Brittany coast at Chaussée de Sein, Finistère. This was a piece of wave-swept, half-submerged granite exposed to the full force of the Atlantic Ocean. In the first two years of the project, workmen succeeded in landing on the rock only twenty-four times and were restricted on each visit to laboring for about an hour before the rising tide forced them to withdraw. It took them an astonishing seven years to establish a cylindrical stone foundation, rooted in the granite with iron bars. Once work on the higher levels of the tower commenced in 1876, progress was more rapid, but the entire project was not completed until fourteen years after it began.

The extreme slowness of the initial progress on the Ar-Men light was exceptional, but a period of two years to establish foundations for a tower was typical. In his account of the building of the Bell Rock lighthouse, Robert Stevenson stated that in 1807, the first year of the project, the number of hours when work was possible added up to only fourteen full days' labor. Most of this time was spent attacking solid rock with pickaxes that barely made a dent and had to be replaced constantly or repaired at an on-site forge. Even at sites above high tide level, initial progress could be tough going. At Tillamook Rock, where the lighthouse was to be placed on a rock 90 feet (27 m) above the sea, it took seven months to prepare the ground for the first stone block to be laid, despite the use of dynamite to level the surface.

Nor was any of the grudging progress the lighthouse builders made necessarily secure. It was not an uncommon experience for the violent onslaught of storms to more or less obliterate the achievement of their initial labors. When French engineer Léonce Reynaud (1803–80) was building the Héaux de Bréhat lighthouse on the Tréguier reef in

Brittany in 1836, he had completed the preparatory work and was about to supervise the laying of the first stone when a three-day storm wrecked the site and took the project almost back to zero. The force that the waves could exert was awesome. On the rock of Dubh Artach (or Dhuheartach) off west Scotland, where engineer Thomas Stevenson (1818-87) was striving to build a lighthouse in 1869, storm waves were powerful enough to sweep eleven stone blocks, each weighing 2 tons, out of the recently laid base of the tower and sink them to the bottom of the ocean.

Conditions for men working on an exposed reef were naturally harsh in the extreme. In a crowded and cramped work area, accidents were frequent – especially fingers and feet crushed by heavy weights – but the sea was the major source of discomfort and menace to life. It is recorded, for example, that during the early stages of building the first Smalls lighthouse in Pembrokeshire, Wales, in the 1770s, the workers frequently had their clothes ripped apart by large waves breaking over their backs and suffered lacerations from being thrown down on the jagged rock. Almost a century later, in the 1860s, conditions for the work gangs building the foundations of the Wolf Rock light (1869) were little different. Alerted by a lookout to the threat of a monster wave arriving, the men would hastily down tools and cling onto safety lines, where they received a thorough battering while their heavy hammers and picks were swept away in the flood like matchsticks.

A watchful eye had to be kept at all times on the state of the weather and the tide, for to be trapped on the rock as the tide inexorably rose would be a terrible fate. Robert Stevenson gave a vivid account of one such dramatic incident at Bell Rock. By mishap, a situation arose in which only two rowboats, each with a capacity of eight men, were at the rock where thirty-two people were working. With the tide rising and soon to cover the rock, and the larger support boat having drifted far off, deaths by drowning seemed imminent. By Stevenson's own account, he did not immediately alert his workmen to the situation because he feared that "a scuffle might have ensued, and it is hard to say...where it might have ended." When the danger at last became evident to all, Stevenson faced a sullen crowd standing "in the most perfect silence." The crisis was resolved by the fortuitous arrival of a supply boat, but it seems that it would not have

Fig. 7.— The lighthouse atop Tillamook Rock, off the coast of Oregon.

Fig. 8.— The remote Scottish Dubh Artach lighthouse, built between 1867 and 1872.

Fig. 9.— At Muckle Flugga light in the Shetlands, a railway was built to bring up provisions.

10.

11.

been the workers' first priority to save their boss, and that he was aware of an underlying antagonism liable to surface in an emergency. On the other hand, the incident underlines the impressive degree to which the engineers shared the danger and discomfort of the enterprise with their workers, which must have been a source of solidarity.

Although the lives of the lighthouse engineers are well documented, it is frustratingly difficult to form a clear picture of the men they employed to work under such harsh conditions. They were not general laborers; each man had his specific job, such as stonemason, blacksmith, carpenter, or pickman. That they were tough men and could be hard to handle is without doubt. At Héaux de Bréhat, Reynaud had to face down a strike by his discontented workers, and at Bell Rock Robert Stevenson implacably snuffed out a mutinous movement to demand a small increase in the exiguous beer ration. Yet Stevenson wrote complacently that "nothing can equal the happy manner in which these excellent workmen spent their time" and "between the tides, they amused themselves in reading, fishing, music, playing cards, draughts [checkers], etc...." No doubt the men needed the pay and made the best of the situation.

As John Smeaton (1724-92) had discovered when building the trailblazing Eddystone light in the late 1750s, the labor force needed to be lodged close to the work site in order to avoid a long daily journey from land and to enable maximum advantage to be taken of favorable weather conditions and tides. In the first stage of building, this usually meant anchoring a boat near the reef for the men to use as temporary accommodation. Being stationed on such a boat - suffering cramped conditions, seasickness, and the dangers of riding close to rocks - was not an experience anyone wished to prolong. So one of the first building tasks was to create a shelter for the workmen alongside the lighthouse site. In addition to living accommodation, this barrack could serve to house a forge needed to repair tools and a kitchen to supply hot food. Such shelters were typically wooden or, at a later date, iron cabins raised on high stilts.

The living space inside these cabins was severely restricted - Robert Stevenson records that his own room in the barrack at Bell Rock, presumably the largest, "did not admit of the full extension of his arms when he stood on the floor." Workers were also exposed to fearsome summer gales.

Fig. 10.— Building La Jument lighthouse off Ushant, Brittany: preparing the foundations in 1906 and fitting the lantern in 1911.

Fig. 11.— Building the Platte Fougère light off Guernsey in the Channel Islands, in c. 1910.

Alan Stevenson, building the Skerryvore lighthouse off the west coast of Scotland between 1838 and 1844, described the experience of spending a night in the wooden barrack at the height of a storm, "our slumbers...fearfully interrupted by the sudden pounding of the sea over the roof, the rocking of the house on its pillars, and the spurting of water through the seams in the doors and windows...." The episode was exceptionally nerve-wracking because a previous wooden barrack built at Skerryvore had been swept away by a storm, fortunately with no one inside it. Alan Stevenson also noted an occasion when "a storm broke and raged for seven weeks almost incessantly, making it impossible for the supply boat to put out...." The men marooned in the barrack faced dwindling food supplies; "fuel was exhausted and worst of all, the supply of tobacco ran out." On one occasion at Dubh Artach, the men were trapped inside their iron barrack for five days while monstrous waves crashed over the roof and seawater swirled through the building. Robert Louis Stevenson, a writer in a family of engineers who witnessed the building of the Dubh Artach light, evocatively described the workmen "high up prisoned in their iron drum, that then resounded with the lashings of the sprays...."

Once a barrack was in place, the rate of construction quickened, but it was not until the base of the tower had risen above the high tide mark that any rapid progress could be made. Working time would then increase from a couple of hours to twelve, fourteen, or even sixteen hours a day, and the working season could be stretched from the summer back into spring and forward into the fall. It was still a dangerous and uncomfortable business laboring in such exposed locations. If bad weather struck, waves might wash right over the top even of a finished lighthouse. But the worst was over once the walls began to rise. The fundamentals of building a stone lighthouse as established by Smeaton remained broadly unchanged until the late 19th century. The stones were prepared at a work site on land, transported by boat, and lifted onto the rock by some form of crane or winch. They were then laid in circular courses to form a tower solid at the base and hollow higher up, where interior space was provided for storerooms and living accommodation. It was a lengthy and laborious operation as the blocks had to be jigsawed together, mortared, and precisely finished, up to a dizzying height – the Skerryvore tower had ninety-seven courses rising

12.

13.

14.

15.

16.

Fig. 12.— Alan Stevenson's magnificent Skerryvore lighthouse in the Hebrides.

Fig. 13.— A light is subjected to an ice shove on Lake Saint Pierre in Quebec.

Fig. 14.— Fourteen Foot Bank light in Delaware Bay, a house on a concrete drum.

Fig. 15.— Building a new lighthouse on Fastnet Rock, Ireland, 1897 to 1904.

Fig. 16.— The new Fastnet lighthouse stands alongside the old tower of 1854.

to 138 feet (42 m). When the final course was laid, there would be a simple ceremony to celebrate the achievement and most of the workers would be paid off. The metal and glass lantern room and cupola were then added on top.

Details of the stone lighthouse altered over time. Smeaton's oak tree shape was revised by the Stevensons into a straighter tower – that is, one with less difference between the circumference at the base and that at the top. Reynaud invented his own variant: a lighthouse with a ponderous lower section and a lighter, slenderer tower on top. He also demonstrated that Smeaton's concern to dovetail the stone blocks had been excessive; a lesser degree of linkage between the blocks proved perfectly effective. But whatever the exact form chosen, every one of these stone lighthouses, rearing smoothly from the tumultuous waves, was an object of exquisite beauty, classical in its simplicity yet romantic in its wild natural setting.

The interiors of the lighthouses were almost universally severe in their stripped-down utilitarianism. A notable exception was the Kéréon lighthouse built off the coast of Brittany between 1907 and 1916 – France's last rock lighthouse. Its construction was partially funded by a personal contribution from descendants of Charles-Marie Le Dall de Kéréon, an aristocratic midshipman who had been guillotined at the age of nineteen during the French Revolution. The money provided a splendid interior with oak-paneled rooms and a marquetry floor of mahogany and ebony, suitable as a memorial for a martyred ancestor. French lighthouse keepers christened it "the palace."

Victorian engineers regarded themselves as hard-headed men engaged in the severely practical business of providing aids to navigation, but the passionate resistance some of them exhibited to the replacement of stone by iron in lighthouse construction must surely have been partly motivated by hidden aesthetic impulses. Yet iron did inevitably come into widespread use in the second half of the 19th century, largely because iron lighthouses were far cheaper and easier to build. There was no reason why metal should not be used to construct a lighthouse to stand on a pier, cliff, or headland, and from the 1840s many such towers were built, swiftly erected on site by relatively unskilled labor from prefabricated parts. But iron was too light to resist the battering of waves if used to build a

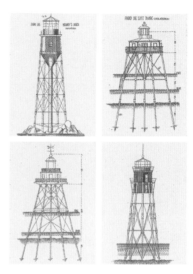

17.

18.

lighthouse in the middle of the sea. This was demonstrated by the fate of the Calf Rock light, an iron tower built on a rock off southwest Ireland in 1866. In a foul Atlantic storm in 1881, the top half of the building was simply swept away.

As a solution to the problem of the use of iron in such challenging locations, engineers conceived structures in which the light would be supported high above the water by piles, the waves hopefully surging harmlessly between the iron legs. But the first attempts to build rock lighthouses in this manner, at Minot's Ledge off the coast of Massachusetts and at Bishop Rock in the Isles of Scilly off southwest England, ended in spectacular failure. Both projects began in 1847 and took three years to complete. While experiencing the usual problems of working hours severely limited by tides and weather, the engineers had holes drilled deep into the rock and iron piles cemented into these holes. The structures raised above this base lacked glamour: the one at Minot's Ledge was described by author Henry Thoreau, observing from the shore, as "an eggshell painted red and placed high on iron pillars, like the ovum of a sea monster floating on the waves." More importantly, they also lacked durability. The iron lighthouse at Bishop Rock was swept away in an Atlantic storm in February 1850, before the light had even been lit; its iron piles had snapped like matchsticks. The Minot's Ledge light lasted until April 1851 before suffering the same fate.

At both Bishop Rock and Minot's Ledge, stone towers were built successfully as replacements for the failed iron structures. But in appropriate circumstances iron-pile designs had a great future, especially in the United States. Screw-pile lighthouses, first introduced in England in the 1840s, proliferated in shallow soft-bottomed inlets such as Chesapeake Bay. The cast-iron screw piles had spiral flanges that twisted into the mud or sand, thereby providing a sufficiently stable base for a structure not too rigorously tested by the elements. However, iron-pile lights were also erected successfully on the coral reefs of the Florida coast, a location exposed to seasonal hurricanes. This was never an easy job. In the first stage of construction, when the iron piles were being driven vertically into the coral, the workers might live in tents on a tiny platform over the reef, a cramped and perilous perch when the sea was rough. During the building of the Fowey Rocks light (1878),

Fig. 17.— Varieties of iron skeleton lighthouses, developed from the 1840s.

Fig. 18.— The iron screw-pile lighthouse at Haneda, Japan, erected in 1875.

Fig. 19.— A lighthouse at One Fathom Bank in the Strait of Malacca, built on steel and concrete piles, nears completion in 1907.

Fig. 20.— The iron screw-pile Fowey Rocks light off the Florida coast entered service in 1878.

Fig. 21.— A cottage-style screw-pile lighthouse at Thimble Shoal in Chesapeake Bay, Virginia.

19.

20.

21.

at the northern end of the Florida reefs, potential heavy loss of life was narrowly averted when the steamship *Arratoon Apcar* ran aground on the reef, missing the workmen's fragile platform by a mere 600 feet (180 m). Once the piles were in place, however, the work progressed with some speed, because the entire superstructure – the keepers' quarters and lantern connected by a spiral staircase enclosed in a metal cylinder – had been prefabricated and test-assembled on land before shipping to the reef. The skeletal cast-iron Fowey Rocks light has since survived many a hurricane and still operates today.

By the later 19th century, new technology was shifting the balance between human capabilities and the elements. The introduction of the pneumatic drill or jackhammer, along with improved explosives, largely removed the need for back-breaking work with pickaxes. Furthermore, the invention of diving suits and oxygen supply for men working under water allowed divers to become part of the lighthouse team. In 1871 to 1874, the building of a lighthouse on the submerged Spectacle Reef on Lake Huron offered an example of the striking new state-of-the-art techniques then coming into operation. Some 10 miles (16 km) from the nearest shore, the location was notably challenging, exposed to violent rollers in summer and to drift ice pushed forward by strong currents in winter. At the start of operations, a square wooden pier or "crib" was towed to the reef by steam tugs and weighted with ballast stones to fix it in place. In the inner space of still water thus created, a hollow metal cylindrical cofferdam was sunk onto the reef. After some preparatory work by divers, the water was pumped out of this cylinder, leaving a dry area below sea level in which the stonemasons could begin work. Living on the wooden pier, the masons built a stone tower in traditional fashion, bolted to the reef and rising course by course to a height of 93 feet (28 m) above the rock, 86 feet (26 m) above water level. The same equipment was reused in the building of the Stannard Rock light on Lake Superior in 1877 to 1883. James Douglass employed a similar cofferdam technique to build the fourth and final Eddystone lighthouse, lit in 1882. And in 1885 German engineers were able to build the Roter Sand lighthouse off Bremerhaven on foundations in the seabed 72 feet (22 m) under water. By the 20th century, it was standard practice to have a massive concrete-filled caisson as the base for a new offshore

22.

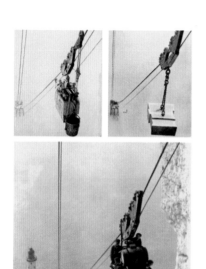

23.

lighthouse; the tower was built on the man-made concrete drum rather than directly on the rock itself.

The Americans coined the term "sparkplug lighthouse" for structures, common in fairly shallow waters around the United States, that consisted of a cylindrical iron tower on top of a caisson - the whole thought to resemble an automobile sparkplug. The iron tower was built on shore and lifted onto the caisson by a crane. Another innovative technique was the use of cableways to carry men and materials. In 1902, a lighthouse was built on a chalk reef at Beachy Head, close to the famous White Cliffs of southern England. A cableway was run 600 feet (182 m) from the lofty clifftop down to the erection site, capable of transporting not only the workers but also stone blocks weighing up to 5 tons.

Whatever the methods employed, building lighthouses on exposed rocks and reefs always required imaginative vision, technological ingenuity, Herculean hard work, and a monumental obstinacy in overcoming setbacks and braving disasters. Each rock lighthouse was in its way an act of faith. It is interesting that Robert Stevenson, a dour God-fearing Scot, made his workers labor on Sundays during the building of the Bell Rock light, arguing that the high purpose they were engaged in justified ignoring the Lord's prescribed day of rest. The lighthouse builder's faith was in progress through the encouragement of commerce and the saving of human lives. From the most modest cottage-style screw-pile lighthouse to the lofty stone towers of the rocky oceanic coasts, the remaining lights today still seem to blaze this essentially hopeful message.

Fig. 22.— Standing alongside the partially dismantled 1872 screw-pile light at Thimble Shoal is the new "sparkplug" light built in 1914, an iron tower on a concrete caisson.

Fig. 23.— Erecting a new lighthouse at Beachy Head, southern England, in 1902, engineers use a cableway to transport men and materials.

1836 ➤ **HOLE IN THE WALL, GUN CAY, CAY SAL | BAHAMAS**

HOLE IN THE WALL (1836), GUN CAY (1836), CAY SAL (1839) ALL DESIGNED BY **CAPTAIN JOHN KITSON** | TOWERS: **CIRCULAR STONE**

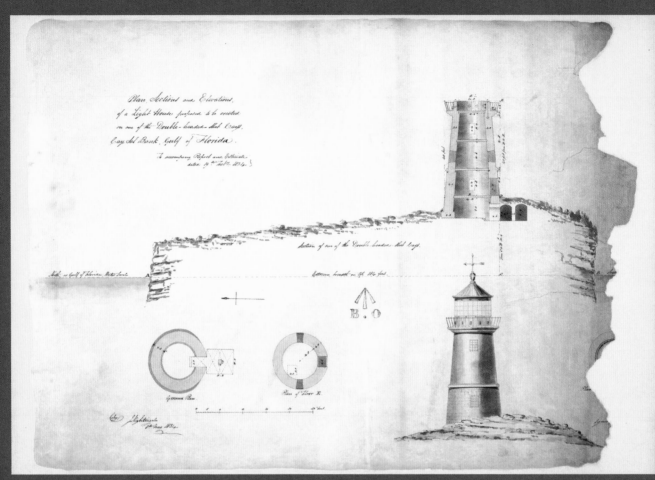

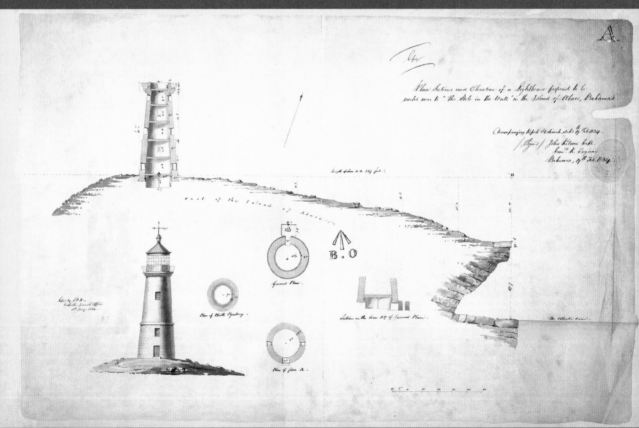

In 1834, British Royal Engineer Captain John Kitson was entrusted with building three lighthouses in the Bahamas, at Hole in the Wall on the southern tip of Great Abaco Island, on Gun Cay in the Bimini Islands, and at Cay Sal on Elbow Cay. These plans show the Cay Sal tower (top), the Hole in the Wall (above), details of the lantern (top right), and the location of the lighthouses, marked in red (bottom right). Kitson did not live to see the lighthouses built, dying of yellow fever in 1835. His wife and children, returning to Britain after his death, were drowned in a shipwreck off Great Abaco.

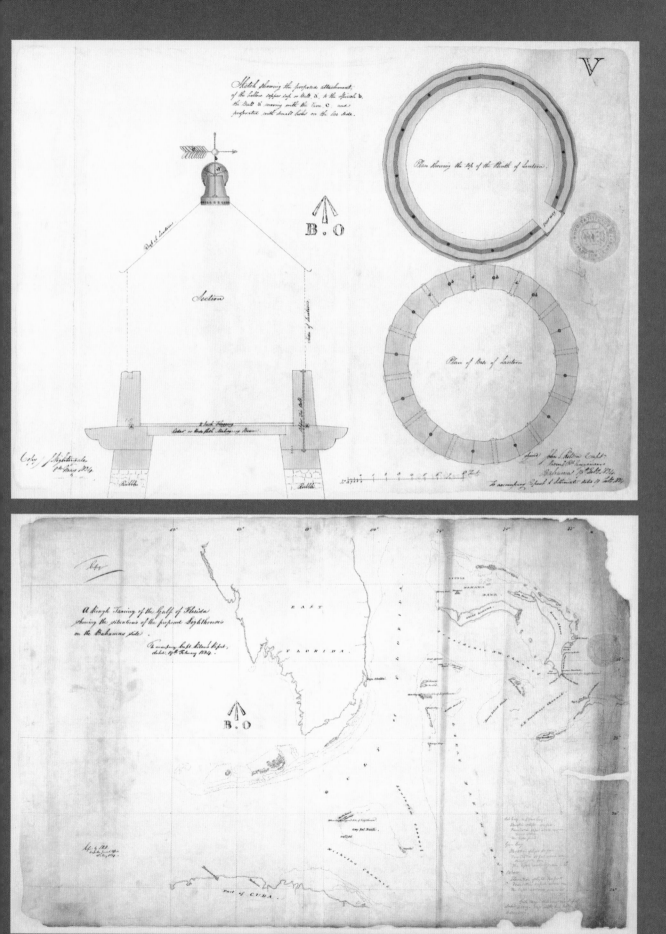

1839 JOMFRULAND
TELEMARK | NORWAY

DESIGNED BY **O. ARNTZEN** | TOWER:
CIRCULAR BRICK | HEIGHT: **102 FT (31 M)**
LIGHT: **OIL LAMPS AND FRESNEL LENS**

PROJECT

til

et Fyrtaarn m. v. paa Jomfruland.

Taarn.

Profil.

Facade.

Plan af Lygten.

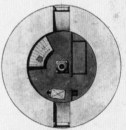

Plan af överste Taarnetage.

Plan af underste Taarnetage.

Christiania 17ᵉ Maij 1836.

Schir

Tegnet af *O Arntzen.*

Nr. 21

74. nr. 2.

The island of Jomfruland lies near the port of Kragerø in Norway's Telemark county. Built there in the 1830s, the lighthouse required 250,000 bricks for its construction, and the lighting system was installed using expertise from France. The drawings shown here were made in 1836. Various floor plans show the entrance hall, the top floor, and the lantern with its balcony. The brick lighthouse functioned for a century before being taken out of service in 1938 when an iron tower was constructed. Although no longer lit, the old brick tower still stands today.

Phares et Balises.

Pl. 20

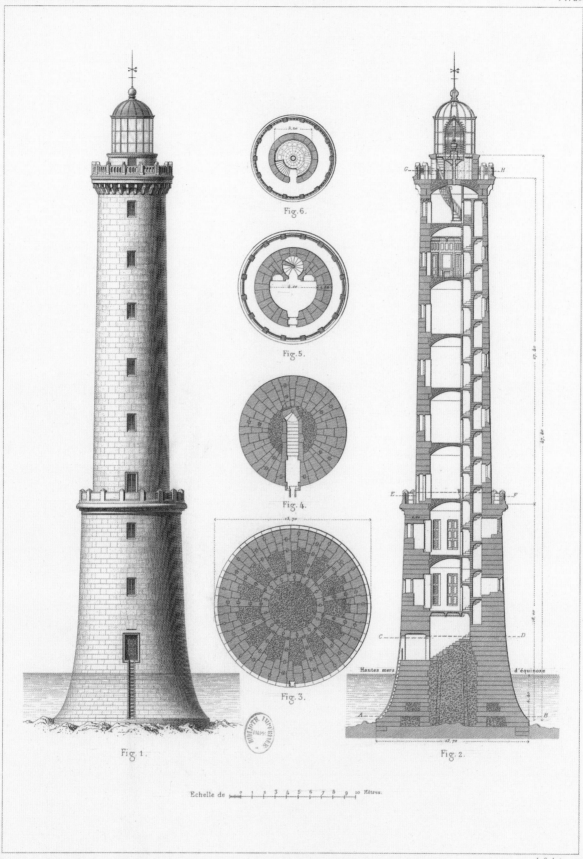

Fig. 6.

Fig. 5.

Fig. 4.

Fig. 3.

Fig. 1.

Fig. 2.

Hautes mers

d'équinoxe

Echelle de .... Mètres.

J. Sulpis sc.

PHARE DE BRÉHAT

In 1834, engineer Léonce Reynaud was entrusted with building a lighthouse on the Tréguier reef, off France's Atlantic coast. He designed a stone structure significantly different from Smeaton's Eddystone or Stevenson's Bell Rock, with a relatively thin-walled, slender column rising from a massive solid masonry base. He also found no need for elaborate dovetailing of the granite blocks. Construction was completed in February 1840 after a heroic six-year struggle with the elements. Blown up by the Germans in World War II, the lighthouse was subsequently rebuilt to its current height of 187 ft (57 m).

PLATE VII.

Stevenson's Account of Skerryvore Lighthouse.

ELEVATION.

Scale of Feet
10 5   0   10   20   30   40   50

James Andrew, Delt.

William Miller, Sculp.

Lying in the Atlantic west of Scotland, 12 miles (19 km)
from the Isle of Tiree, Skerryvore reef was a notorious hazard
to shipping. For this exposed location, Alan Stevenson
designed the tallest lighthouse tower yet built in modern
times. Construction of a barrack for workers at the site began
in 1838 but the first stones - granite from the Isle of Mull - were
not laid until 1840. The light, a novel custom-built version of
a Fresnel lens, was finally lit in 1844. Alan Stevenson's nephew,
Robert Louis Stevenson, described the gracefully tapering tower
as "the noblest of all extant deep-sea lights."

N.º III.

PLAN OF SKERRYVORE ROCK
AT HIGH WATER OF SPRING TIDES.

Scale of Feet

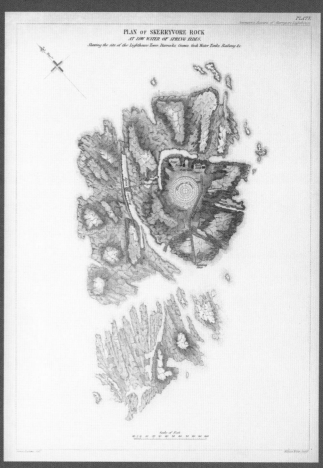

PLATE

PLAN OF SKERRYVORE ROCK
AT LOW WATER OF SPRING TIDES.
Shewing the site of the Lighthouse Tower, Barracks, Crane, Fresh Water Tanks, Railway &c.

Scale of Feet

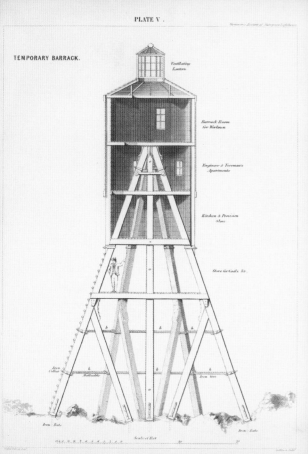

PLATE V.

TEMPORARY BARRACK.

Ventilating Lantern

Barrack Room for Workmen

Engineer & Foreman's Apartments

Kitchen & Provision Store

Store for Coals &c

Iron Collar
Malleable
Iron Tree

Iron Bats
Iron Bats

Scale of Feet

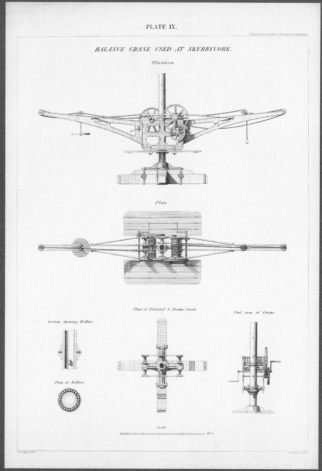

PLATE IX.

BALANCE CRANE USED AT SKERRYVORE.

Elevation

Plan

Section shewing Rollers

Plan of Pedestal & Frame Circle

End view of Crane

Plan of Rollers

Scale

69

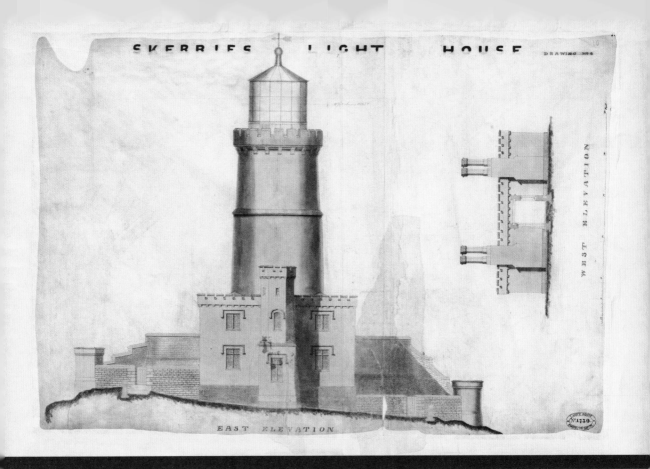

SKERRIES LIGHT HOUSE

DRAWING Nº 4

WEST ELEVATION

EAST ELEVATION

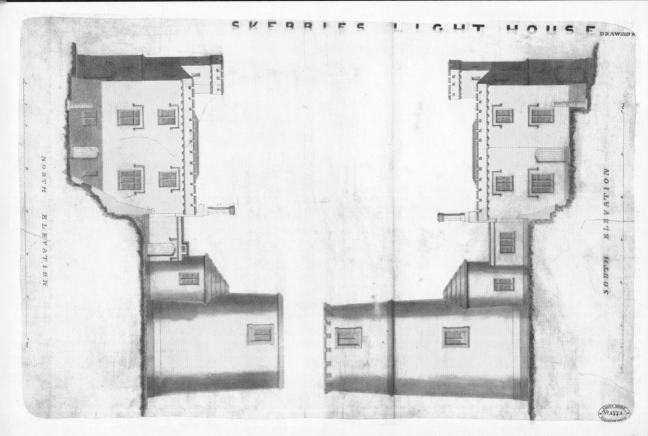

SKERRIES LIGHT HOUSE

DRAWING N

NORTH ELEVATION

SOUTH ELEVATION

The Skerries rocks lie 4 miles (6.5 km) off the coast of Anglesey, and are a menace to shipping using the ports of Holyhead and Liverpool. The first lighthouse tower was built there in 1717 by William Trench, replaced by a new tower in 1759. This privately owned lighthouse was bought by Trinity House in 1841 for £444,984, which was a phenomenal sum of money at that time. Trinity House had the building extensively updated by engineer James Walker. His innovations included a new crenellated parapet and a cast-iron lantern containing sixteen Argand lamps and reflectors.

SKERRIES LIGHT HOUSE

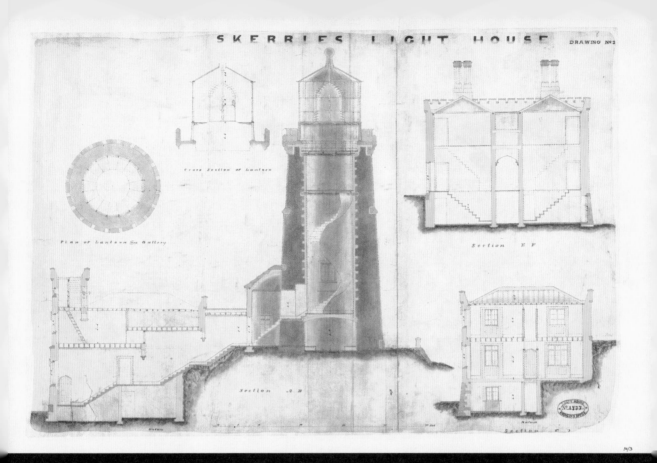

Cross Section of Lantern

Plan of Lantern and Gallery

Section E F

Section A B

Section C D

SKERRIES LIGHT HOUSE

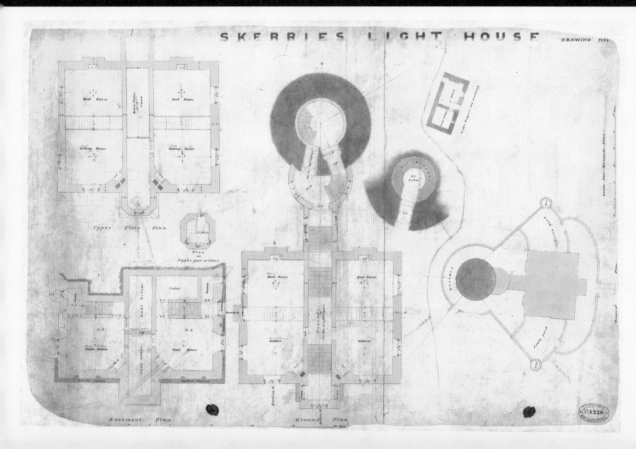

Upper Floor Plan.

Plan of Upper part of Tower

Basement Plan

Ground Plan

1850 > MINOT'S LEDGE
MASSACHUSETTS | USA

FIRST LIGHTHOUSE DESIGNED BY **CAPTAIN WILLIAM
H. SWIFT** IN **1850** | TOWER: **IRON SKELETAL** | HEIGHT:
70 FT (21 M) | LIGHT: **OIL LAMPS AND REFLECTORS**

Nov. 1849 –
Established 1850 – 1 Jan
Destroyed 1851 16 April

2.ᵈ Dist.
3 M.

Work on building a lighthouse at Minot's Ledge, a dangerous reef on the approaches to Boston Harbor, began in 1847. Instead of a stone tower, a revolutionary iron skeletal design was chosen. Nine wrought-iron piles were cemented into solid rock, supporting at their summit keepers' accommodation and the lantern. The light was lit at the start of 1850. It was argued that the skeletal iron tower would survive the battering of the ocean better than a solid structure. However, keepers soon reported an alarming tendency of the tower to sway. In April 1851, the lighthouse was swept away in a storm.

After the collapse of the first Minot's Ledge lighthouse, the newly established Lighthouse Board adopted a traditional stone lighthouse design for the site. US Army engineers were responsible for the second lighthouse, designed by Colonel Totten and executed by Captain Barton S. Alexander as on-site engineer. The painfully slow work on the foundations began in 1855, and the first stone courses were laid in 1858. The tower, made of dovetailed granite blocks, was solid up to a height of 40 ft (12 m). Entering service in November 1860, it has survived over a century and a half of battering by the waves.

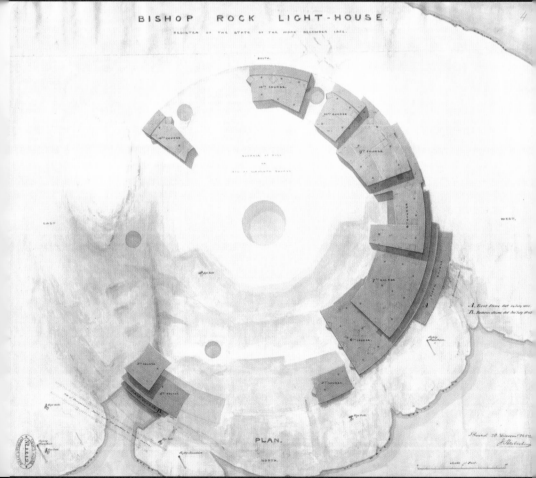

BISHOP ROCK LIGHT-HOUSE

REGISTER OF THE STATE OF THE WORK DECEMBER 1852.

PLAN.

Bishop Rock is one of the most exposed locations on which a lighthouse has ever been built, a tiny wave-swept island at the southwestern extremity of England, receiving the full force of the Atlantic Ocean. Trinity House engineer James Walker began the attempt to build an iron skeletal lighthouse on this site in 1847 (above, top). His calculations proved seriously awry. By 1850 the tower had been built but the light had not yet been installed. A fierce February storm snapped the iron legs like sticks and the lighthouse was swept away, fortunately with no one in residen

SECOND LIGHTHOUSE DESIGNED BY **JAMES WALKER** IN **1858** | TOWER: **CIRCULAR STONE** HEIGHT: **147 FT (45 M)** | LIGHT: **UNKNOWN**

THIRD LIGHTHOUSE DESIGNED BY **JAMES DOUGLASS** IN **1887** | TOWER: **CIRCULAR STONE** HEIGHT: **160 FT (49 M)** LIGHT: **CHANCE HYPERRADIAL**

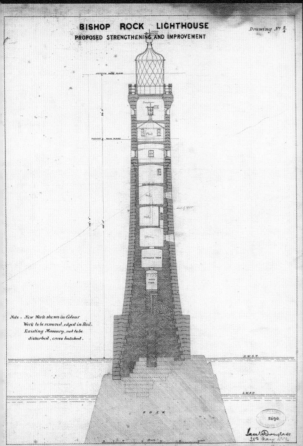

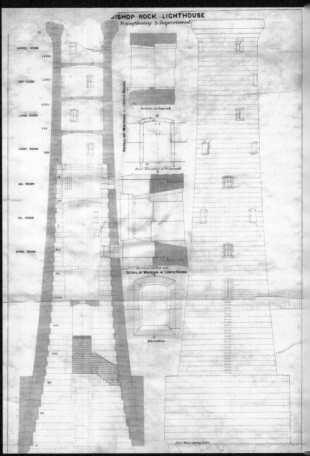

Undeterred by the failure of his iron structure, Walker began work on a second Bishop Rock lighthouse in 1851 (opposite, bottom, and above, top left and right). Made of dovetailed Cornish granite blocks, it was solid to a height of 45 ft (14 m). The lighthouse entered service in 1858, but soon showed

signs of being vulnerable to storms. In 1883, work began on strengthening and heightening the structure. Designed by James Douglass and executed by his son William, the upgrade encased the tower in an extra layer of masonry and added a cylindrical platform at the base (above, bottom left and right).

BISHOP ROCK LIGHTHOUSE

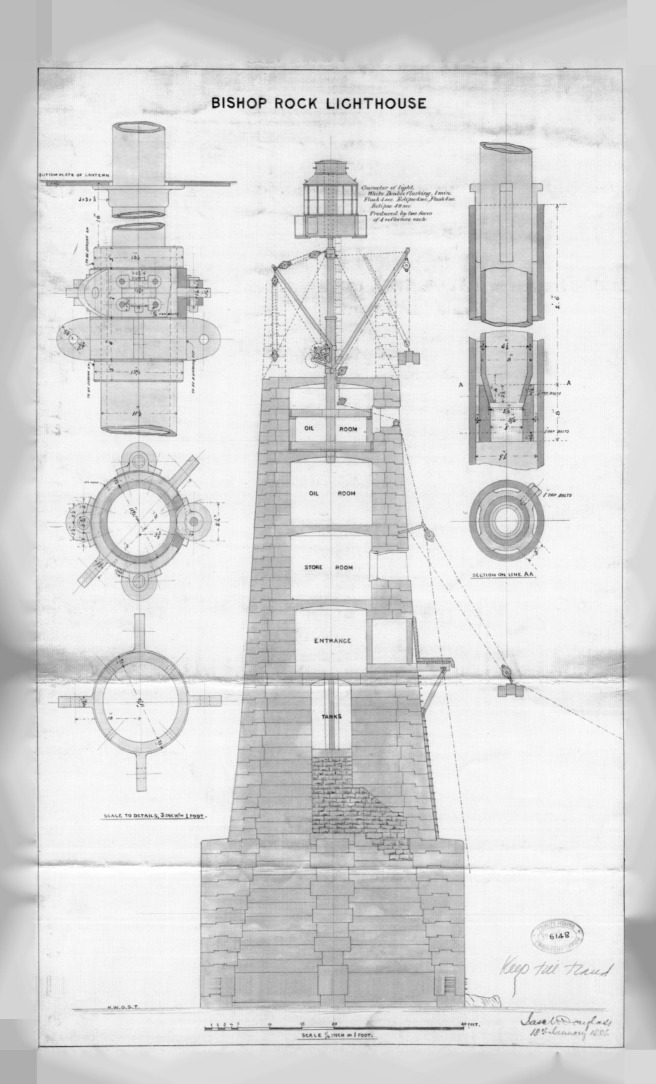

Character of light.
White Double flashing, 1 min.
Flash 4 sec. Eclipse 4 sec, Flash 4 sec.
Eclipse 48 sec.
Produced by two faces
of 4 reflectors each.

BOTTOM PLATE OF LANTERN

OIL   ROOM

OIL   ROOM

STORE   ROOM

ENTRANCE

TANKS

SECTION ON LINE AA.

SCALE TO DETAILS, 3 INCH = 1 FOOT.

H.W.O.S.T.

SCALE ¼ INCH = 1 FOOT.

Keep till traced

Jas N Douglass
18th January 1886.

BISHOP ROCK LIGHTHOUSE.

Service Room

Lantern Floor and Gallery

Living Room

Bed Room

Water Room.

Store Room

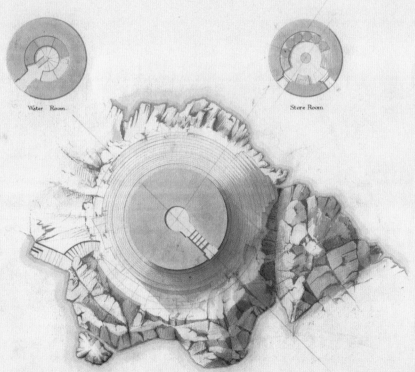

Plan at Entrance Door.

Scale of Feet

Jas N Douglass
29th November 188[?]

LIGHT HOUSE FOR SHELL KEYS, La.

Scale ⅛ or ¼ inch to the Foot.

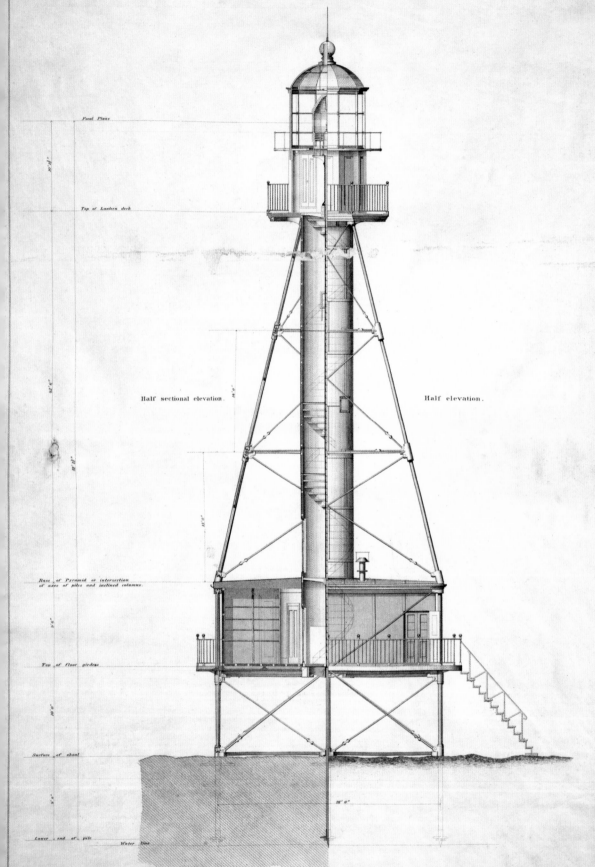

Half sectional elevation.

Half elevation.

Scale of feet.

Focal Plane

Top of Lantern deck

Base of Pyramid or intersection of axes of piles and inclined columns.

Top of floor girders

Surface of shoal

Lower end of pile

Water line

LIGHT HOUSE FOR SHELL KEYS, La.
Foundation Screw.
Drawn half Size

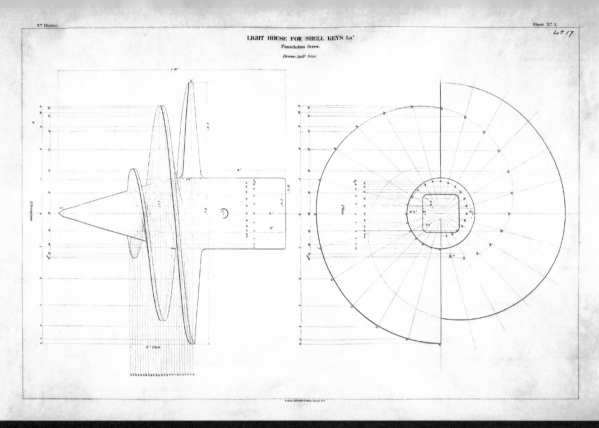

LIGHT HOUSE FOR SHELL KEYS, La.
Details of Lantern.

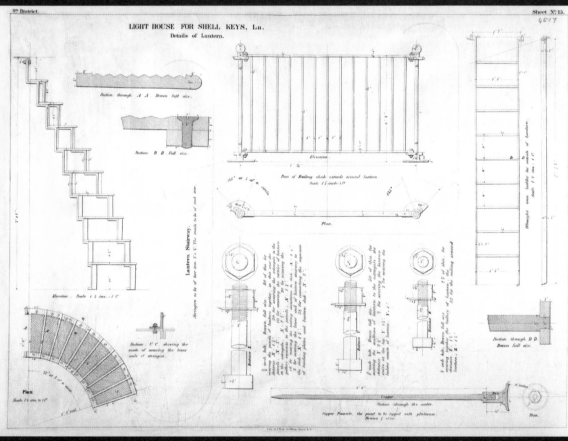

Built offshore at the entrance to Vermilion Bay, Shell Keys was a typical US iron screw-pile lighthouse of its day. The legs of the tower ended in cast-iron screws with spiral flanges that were screwed into the soft seabed. The skeletal iron structure was designed to present minimal resistance to wind and waves.

A central stair cylinder gave access to the lantern. Although in general screw-pile lighthouses were successful off the southern United States, the Shell Keys light was destroyed by a hurricane in 1867, causing the death of lighthouse keeper Seth Jones.

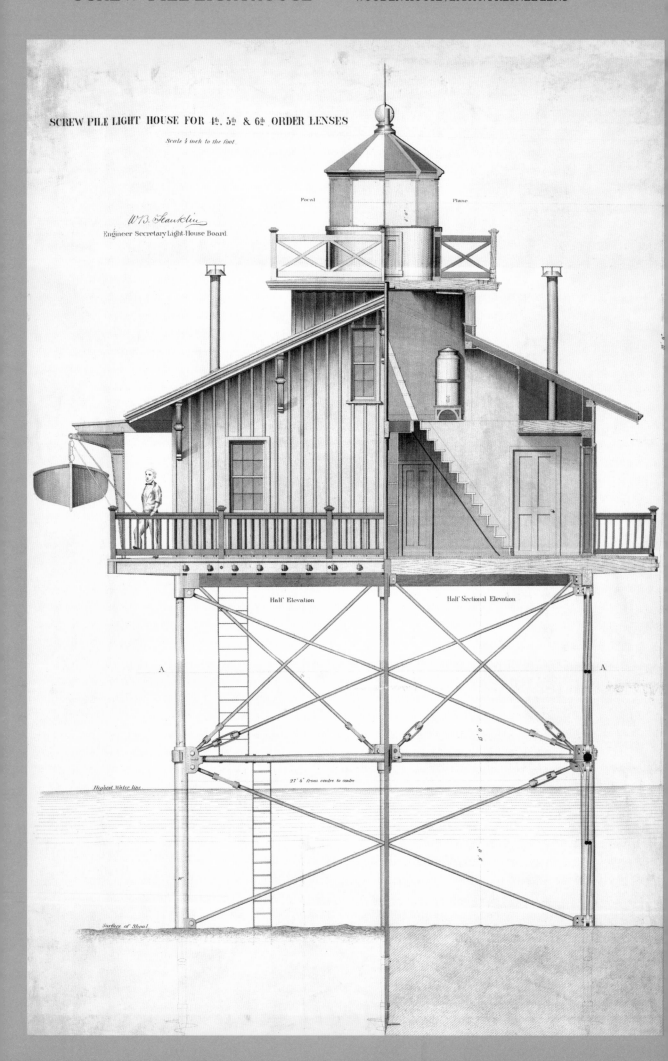

From 1857 to 1859, Captain William B. Franklin was Army Engineer Secretary of the US Lighthouse Board. The Board had undertaken to build large numbers of new lighthouses with Fresnel lenses, but there were also the usual pressures to keep down costs. Franklin devised this design for a cheap easy-to-build style of lighthouse, with iron piles supporting a wooden house with an iron-and-glass lantern, suitable for a Fresnel lens, on its roof. Known as "cottage-style" lighthouses, numerous variants on this design were built in US coastal waters from the 1850s.

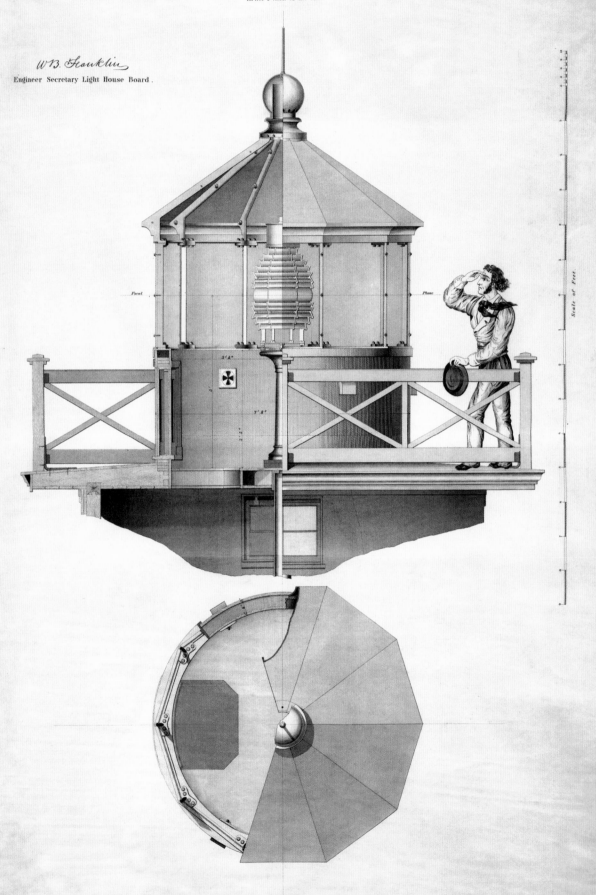

SCREW PILE LIGHT HOUSE FOR 4th, 5th & 6th ORDER LENSES.

Scale 1 inch to the foot.

W.B. Franklin
Engineer Secretary Light House Board.

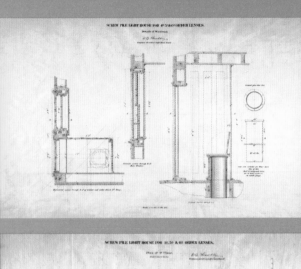

SCREW PILE LIGHT HOUSE FOR 4 5 & 6 ORDER LENSES.

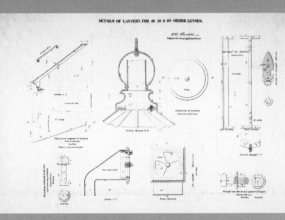

DETAILS OF LANTERN FOR 4 5 & 6 ORDER LENSES.

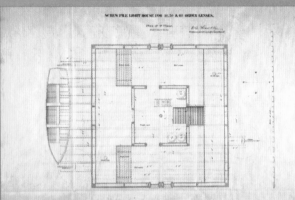

SCREW PILE LIGHT HOUSE FOR 4 5 & 6 ORDER LENSES.

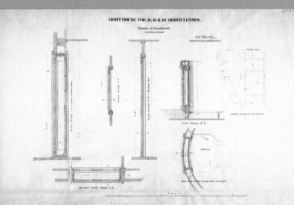

LIGHT HOUSE FOR 4 5 & 6 ORDER LENSES.

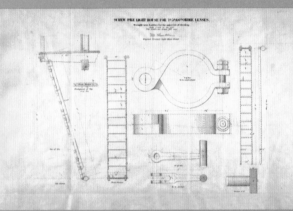

SCREW PILE LIGHT HOUSE FOR 4 5 & 6 ORDER LENSES.

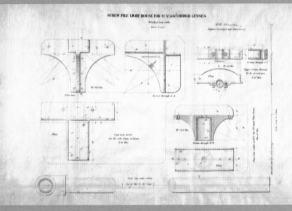

SCREW PILE LIGHT HOUSE FOR 4 5 & 6 ORDER LENSES.

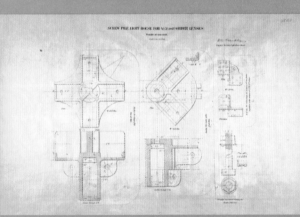

SCREW PILE LIGHT HOUSE FOR 4 5 & 6 ORDER LENSES.

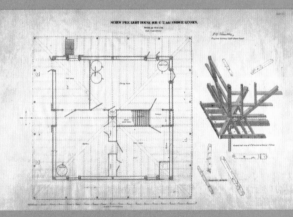

SCREW PILE LIGHT HOUSE FOR 4 5 & 6 ORDER LENSES.

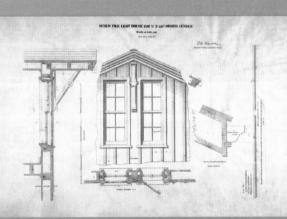

SCREW PILE LIGHT HOUSE FOR 4 5 & 6 ORDER LENSES.

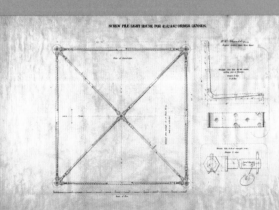

SCREW PILE LIGHT HOUSE FOR 4 5 & 6 ORDER LENSES.

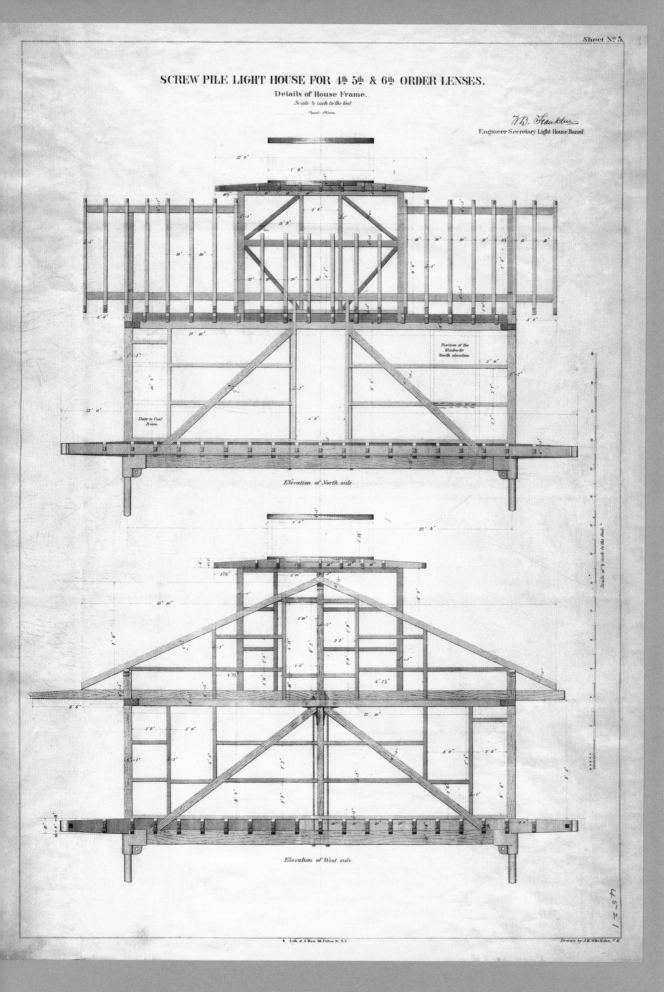

The one-and-a-half-story wooden frame cottage was designed to provide living accommodation for two keepers and space for the storage of fuel and drinking water. The first floor was divided into a bedroom, sitting room, kitchen, and storeroom. The second floor had a bedroom and the oil room. Access to the house from the sea was by iron ladders. The house in Franklin's design is square, but most cottage-style lighthouses were hexagonal, including Maryland's Thomas Point Shoal Light (1875). This style of lighthouse proved vulnerable to extreme weather, especially ice, and none were built after 1910.

CHAPTER 3.

A

LIGHT IN THE

DARKNESS.

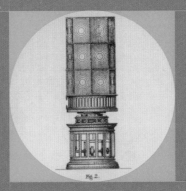

Fig. 2.

THE EVOLUTION OF

LIGHTS AND LENSES.

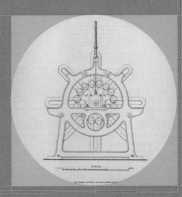

1.

It is hard for us today to imagine how dark the night must once have been. In the 18th century, when the modern era of lighthouse building got under way, even the largest cities were sparsely lit. The flickering light of tallow candles or primitive smoky oil lamps, the occasional blaze of an open fire or flambeau put up scattered and feeble resistance to the enveloping darkness. The few beacons for sailors maintained on towers and headlands were usually braziers in which wood or coal was burned, consuming large quantities of fuel and useless in bad weather. For example, the open wood fire atop Estonia's Baltic Kõpu lighthouse (1531) used so much fuel it caused deforestation on the peninsula where it stood, yet was still unreliable because it was frequently extinguished by wet weather. The use of coal as a fuel had become common in lighthouses around the North Sea and Baltic by the 17th century, and the Germans and Dutch in particular built square towers known as "Steinkohlblüse," where a bellows served to improve the effectiveness of the coal fire. But the result remained unsatisfactory. The state of marine illumination had not improved notably by the time John Smeaton (1724-92) completed his groundbreaking work, the Eddystone lighthouse, in 1759. The most advanced illumination Smeaton could find to place in its lantern was a chandelier mounting twenty-four candles.

Swiss inventor Aimé Argand (1750-1803) is credited with developing the lamp that first revolutionized marine lights. Argand was an active figure in the European Enlightenment, involved in the Montgolfier brothers' early experiments with balloon flights in France and acquainted with steam engine pioneers James Watt and Matthew Boulton in Britain. Developed in the 1780s, his Argand lamp had a wick shaped like a hollow cylinder, enclosed in a glass chimney. It produced a light four times brighter than any previous oil lamp and, when it first appeared, amazed everyone who saw it. Running best on sperm oil, it initially helped promote the wholesale slaughter of whales, although canola oil and other vegetable oils were soon found to be a cheaper fuel for the lamps.

The Argand lamp's potential for use in lighthouses was perceived immediately, but to make the first truly effective beam it needed a mirror to concentrate its light. Any reflective surface placed behind any kind of light would enhance its brightness to some degree, but parabolic mirrors

OPPOSITE

Top: Diagram of the twenty-eight-jet gas burner designed by John R. Wigham.

Center: A triform gas burner, consisting of three twenty-eight-jet burners stacked on top of one another.

Center right: Diagram showing the vertical placement of lenses for triform revolving gas lights.

Bottom left: The four-wick cylindro-conical burner used in French lighthouses toward the end of the 1860s.

Bottom center: Transverse section of the machine room at La Hève, France, showing the engine and "magneto-electric machine."

Bottom right: Side elevation of the "magneto-electric machine" at La Hève, France. It produced electricity to power the light by means of steam engines.

ABOVE

Fig. 1.— A design for a lighthouse with an external spiral staircase, 1815.

were recognized as having the best potential to concentrate the rays from a lamp in a single direction. Creating the exact kind of parabolic mirror to produce the optimum effect with an oil lamp was, however, far from easy, as was manufacturing such mirrors to fine tolerances. Thomas Smith (1752-1814), the man appointed the first chief engineer of the Scottish Northern Lighthouse Board, was a lamp maker who had lit the streets of Edinburgh's New Town with oil lamps backed by burnished copper mirrors. This was, in effect, his qualification for the job. His lighthouse at Kinnaird Head, first lit in 1787, had seventeen whale-oil lamps with parabolic reflectors and was said to be the most powerful light of its day. This combination of oil lamps and mirrors, grandiloquently dubbed the "catoptric" system, had established itself as the world's cutting-edge lighthouse illumination by the early 19th century.

Despite valiant efforts in Scotland and elsewhere, there is no doubt that the French led the way in the development of lighthouse lamps and optics. France did not necessarily have better scientists, but it did have better links between science, government, and civil engineering. Scientists were taken seriously and found ready financial and bureaucratic support to put their ideas into practice. Thus it was that Augustin-Jean Fresnel (1788-1827), a scientist engaged in the study of light waves and optics, was appointed to a senior position in the French state lighthouse organization in 1819, when neither the British Trinity House nor the US Lighthouse Service had a single genuine man of science on board. Specifically tasked with inventing an improved light, Fresnel devised the lens that bears his name - arguably the most radical single breakthrough in the entire history of lighthouses. The Fresnel lens was an optical device of astounding complexity and refinement. It consisted of a bull's eye lens at the center of rings of pyramidal crystals that augmented its effect. The largest Fresnel lens stood 12 feet (3.6 m) tall, weighed 6,000 pounds (2,720 kg), and comprised more than a thousand crystal prisms, each finished to a high level of precision. Combined with the Fresnel four-wick oil lamp, this nest of glass refractors was able to concentrate by far the most powerful beam of light yet seen. The first Fresnel lens was installed atop the historic Cordouan lighthouse in 1823 and it quickly became standard issue in French lighthouses.

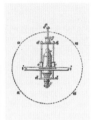

2.

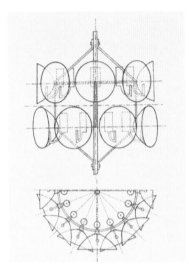

3.

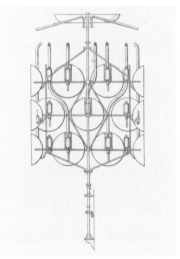

4.

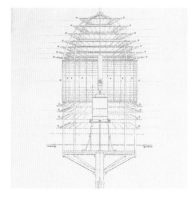

5.

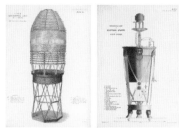

6.

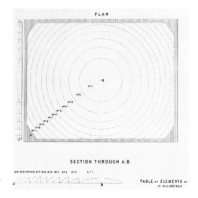

7.

Fig. 2.— An oil fountain supplies fuel to an Argand lamp with a parabolic reflector.

Fig. 3.— The fixed catoptric system was an immobile series of oil lamps and reflectors.

Fig. 4.— The revolving catoptric apparatus was state of the art in the early 19th century.

Fig. 5.— The beehive-shaped Fresnel lens revolutionized lighthouse illumination.

Fig. 6.— Fresnel lenses work with any light source, including a gas burner.

Fig. 7.— The Fresnel device has concentric glass rings around a central lens.

Fresnel lenses had a great future in diverse spheres – from car headlights to movie projectors – but their use in lighthouses was quite slow to spread beyond the borders of France. They were staggeringly expensive to make and, at first, were manufactured only by French firms. Initially Britain lacked any company with sufficient glassmaking skills or know-how in optics to make a Fresnel lens. After considerable hesitation, Alan Stevenson (1807-65) adopted the new system and placed a French-manufactured Fresnel light in his Skerryvore lighthouse in 1842. Eventually, the supply problem was cracked by a Birmingham firm, Chance Brothers, which provided the glass for the renowned Crystal Palace that housed London's Great Exhibition of 1851. In the second half of the 19th century, Chance grew to be the world's leading supplier of lights for lighthouses, chiefly marketing Stevenson-adapted versions of the Fresnel system.

In the United States, an initial failure to adopt the Fresnel lens became a public issue that pitted merchants and sailors against the parsimony of the federal lighthouse service. US lighthouses were fitted with a version of the catoptric system devised by former sea captain Winslow Lewis. It combined an Argand lamp, a mirror, and a lens; the lens, like a lump of green bottle glass, to a large degree negated the effectiveness of the lamp and mirror. The inadequacy of these lights was obvious to mariners. A US naval officer once denounced the lighthouse at Cape Hatteras (1803) on North Carolina's Outer Banks as "the worst light in the world." US Commodore Matthew Perry was sent by Congress in 1838 to bring back Fresnel lenses from Paris to be tried out, and they passed the test with flying colors, but the Fresnel system was not finally adopted in the United States until the creation of the Lighthouse Board in 1852. Take-up of the new light was then remarkably energetic and thorough; most US lighthouses sported Fresnel lenses by the end of the decade. During the Civil War (1861-65), these valuable high-tech optical devices became the target of military action.

By the later 19th century, some lights of extraordinary power were being deployed in key locations. The Galley Head lighthouse in County Cork, Ireland, first lit in 1878, had a coal gas light delivering around a million candlepower, visible over 16 nautical miles (29 km). Hyperradiant (or hyperradial) lenses of the kind installed in the Makapuu Point lighthouse on Oahu island, Hawaii, in 1909 far surpassed even a first-order Fresnel lens in size and complexity. The Makapuu Point light is reckoned to be visible at a distance of 19 nautical miles (35 km).

As lighthouses proliferated around the world's coastlines, another problem came to the fore. It was not enough for sailors that a light should be visible; it also needed to be identifiable. Confusing one light with another could lead to fatal errors of navigation. As early as 1781, Swedish engineer Jonas Norberg (1711-83) installed a revolving light at Carlsten in Sweden. He used a clockwork mechanism to rotate a frame carrying three oil lamps and six parabolic reflectors, creating a pattern of six strong flashes every five minutes, with a weaker light always in view. Variants on this quite simple system, including the additional use of shades to block the light intermittently as required, proved extremely effective over the years, generating sufficient different patterns of flashes or swelling and fading light to individually distinguish large numbers of lighthouses.

Typically, the rotating mechanism was modeled on large clocks of the period. Heavy weights hanging on chains were attached to a system of gears. Every few hours, the lighthouse keeper laboriously wound a handle to raise the weights, which then slowly descended, rotating the light as they went. The weights moved up and down inside a long metal tube at the center of the lighthouse tower. This weight tube, in the middle of every floor of the building, was an added obstruction to the keepers living and working in an already restricted space. As the lights increased in size and thus became more ponderous, thought had to be given to improving the efficiency of the rotation. The ingenious solution was to place the light on a pedestal that floated in a circular trough of mercury. Resistance was reduced to such a minimal quantity that a light weighing more than 10 tons could be moved by the touch of a finger.

Rotation was not enough to allow all sea lights to be identifiable individually. It was necessary to introduce color into the equation if sufficient variety were to be achieved. Joseph Huddart (1741-1816), a British engineer elected to the Elder Brethren of Trinity House in 1791, is credited as the first man to advocate the use of colored glass with a catoptric reflector, an idea then taken up by Robert Stevenson (1772-1850). In practice, red was found to be the only truly effective color at any great distance and even that severely reduced the power of the original white light, as the interposed red shade or glass filtered out more than half the rays. Still, patterns of

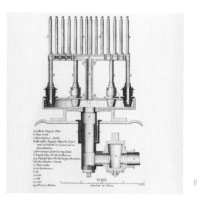

8.

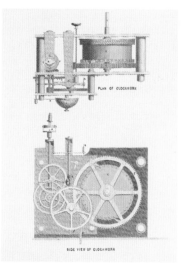

PLAN OF CLOCKWORK

SIDE VIEW OF CLOCKWORK

9.

10.

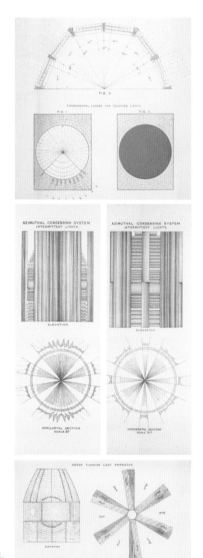

Fig. 8.— Coal gas burner in use at Galley Head lighthouse in Ireland from 1878.

Fig. 9.— The clockwork gears controlling the rotating mechanism on a light.

Fig. 10.— Kampen lighthouse in North Frisia, one of the first to use petroleum.

Fig. 11.— Alan Stevenson's technical drawings of lights, including flashing and revolving systems.

red and white light, added to the periodic flashing, rendered confusion between lights rare.

The technology of lighthouse illumination never stood still, although cost considerations were always liable to put some restraint on innovation. Many relatively archaic lights long remained in operation because they were considered "good enough." An electric carbon arc light was installed in the South Foreland lighthouse near Dover in southern England as early as 1858, but the adoption of electricity was slow because it was seen as simply too expensive. Mineral oils such as kerosene (paraffin) widely replaced vegetable oils during the second half of the 19th century because they were both efficient and cheap. The Kampen lighthouse on the German island of Sylt (then under Danish rule) was one of the first to employ petroleum as a fuel in 1856. The incandescent gas mantle, invented by Austrian scientist Carl Auer von Welsbach (1858-1929) and first manufactured in the 1890s, also found its way into many lighthouses.

The extraordinary Swedish inventor Gustaf Dalén (1869-1937) entered lighthouse history as chief engineer of the Swedish AGA company in the early 20th century. People who identify AGA with fuel-efficient ovens may be surprised to learn that it made its initial reputation building lighthouses. The Swedish lighthouse authorities at the time faced a daunting problem creating and maintaining sea lights for their long coast lined with clusters of islands and rocky islets. What they needed were unmanned lights that would require minimum maintenance. The inventive Dalén found a way of fulfilling this need using the dangerously explosive gas acetylene. Acetylene was potentially an ideal fuel for marine lights, since it gave off a white radiance so bright it could dispense with the elaborate optics being employed to boost other light sources. In 1906, Dalén invented an acetylene lamp, with the gas stored in cylinders and an automatic control device known as a "sun valve." A trigger activated by daylight falling on copper bars automatically switched the gas supply on at dusk and off at dawn. Another control valve made the light flash, turning off the gas between flashes. Dalén even created a clockwork mechanism to change the lamp's mantle periodically, as mantles would deteriorate over time. The result of these inventions was an economical, unmanned lighthouse that needed to be visited only twice a year. Dalén lights were

12.

13.

14.

15.

Fig. 12.— The first-order Fresnel lens light installed at Point Reyes, California, in 1870.

Fig. 13.— Fog siren at Fort Doyle, Guernsey.

Fig. 14.— Daboll foghorn protrudes from the engine house at Cape Cod's Highland light.

Fig. 15.— Daboll foghorn, Southwest Ledge light, New Haven, Connecticut.

soon proliferating across the world, from the Panama Canal to the coast of Zanzibar. Tragically, Dalén was blinded in an explosion while experimenting with acetylene in 1912, shortly before being awarded the Nobel Prize in Physics in recognition of his lighthouse work.

However powerful the lights deployed to mark coasts and reefs, they could never penetrate dense fog. Although some ingenuity was shown in devising techniques for warning mariners in poor visibility, these long remained relatively primitive and improvised. Up to the mid 19th century, the available technology consisted chiefly of fog bells and of fog guns firing blanks. In the 1850s, a US inventor, Celadon Leeds Daboll (1818-66), devised a foghorn known as the Daboll trumpet. A coal fire heated air in a cylinder, forcing it to exit over a steel reed into a huge horn 17 feet (5 m) long and more than 6 feet (1.8 m) wide at its open end. Only a limited number of Daboll trumpets ever entered service - the Canadian lighthouse authorities, after trials, rejected them as unreliable and "sources of danger instead of aids to navigation" - but they initiated the age of the foghorn. Many varieties were produced in the second half of the 19th century, mostly steam driven, and their mournful bellow became a familiar part of the soundtrack of life in coastal communities. In 1903, Robert Hope-Jones (1859-1914), the inventor of the Wurlitzer theater organ, introduced the diaphone, using compressed air and a piston to generate an extremely powerful and consistent sound. First installed in Canada along the Great Lakes waterways, diaphones became common throughout North America and beyond. All foghorns were substantial equipment, requiring their own buildings alongside the lighthouse. Where no room was available for such installations - that is, at many rock lighthouses - various forms of explosive charge still had to be set off as audible warnings in fog.

From World War I onward, lighthouses ceased to be the focus of inventiveness and innovation, instead benefiting from a wave of technological improvements devised for other purposes. First telephones, radios, electric motors, and electric timers, then radar, remote radio-control, and GPS transformed the operation of lighthouses and navigation. But by this time, the lighthouse was being towed along in the wake of progress rather than standing at the prow.

1861 ROMAN ROCK
SIMON'S TOWN | S. AFRICA

DESIGNED BY **ALEXANDER GORDON** | TOWER: **IRON**
ON CIRCULAR STONE PEDESTAL | HEIGHT: **46 FT (14 M)**
ORIGINAL LIGHT: **OIL LAMPS AND REFLECTORS**

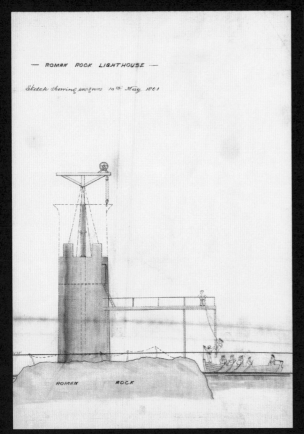

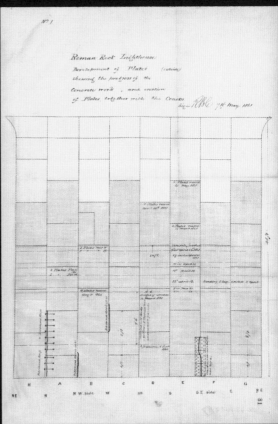

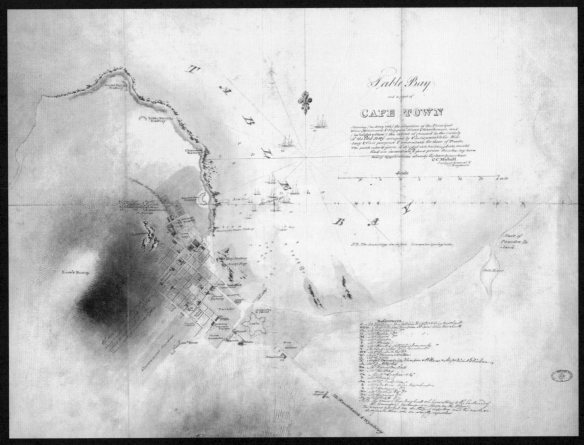

OPPOSITE The original Montauk Point lighthouse was built at the eastern extremity of Long Island in 1797, its thick walls made with sandstone from Connecticut. In 1860, it was upgraded in the form shown here, extended in height from 80 ft (24 m) to 110 ft (33 m) and installed with a Fresnel lens.

ABOVE The design for the lighthouse on a rock in False Bay, off the coast at Simon's Town, called for a base of locally quarried granite, on which a prefabricated iron tower would be erected. Building the pedestal in mid-ocean was a painfully slow process, and the whole project took four years to complete.

LIGHT HOUSE FOR CAPE ANN, MASS.

Capt. W.B. Franklin. Engineer.

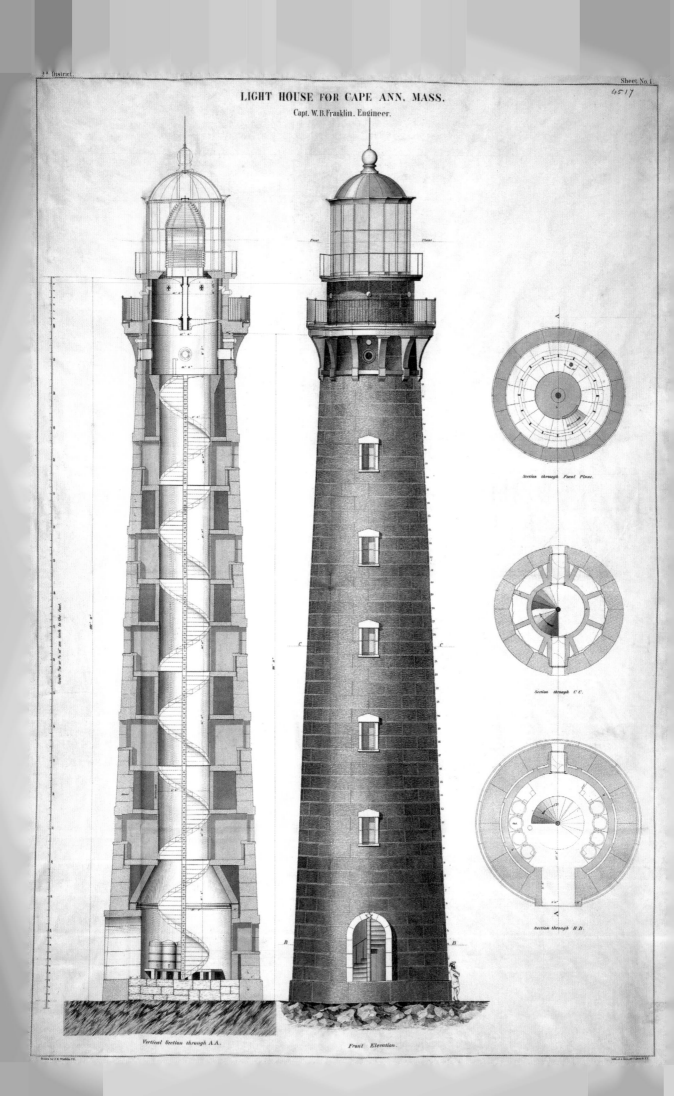

Section through Front Plane.

Section through C.C.

Section through B.B.

Vertical Section through A.A.

Front Elevation.

LIGHT HOUSE FOR CAPE ANN Mass.

Details

Scale ⅛ in = 1ft

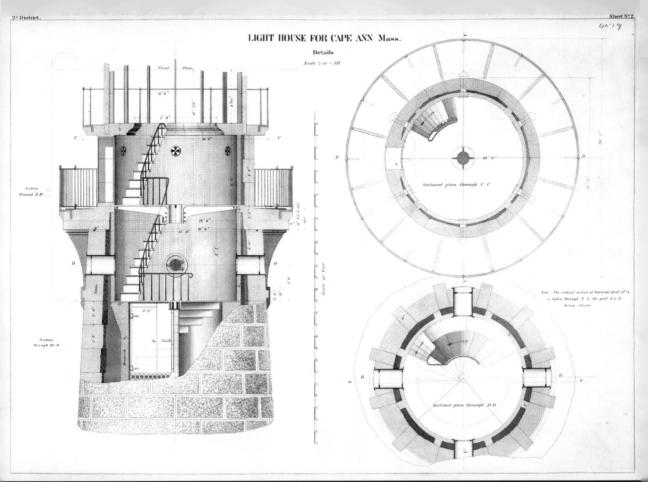

LIGHT HOUSE FOR CAPE ANN Mass.

Details

Scale ¾ or 3 ins = 1ft

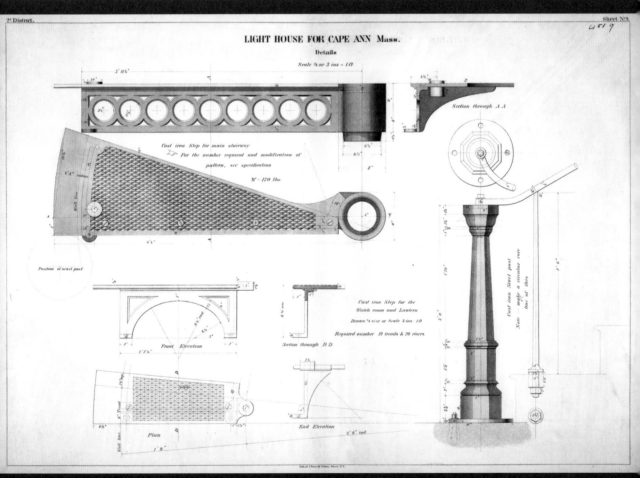

The twin lighthouses built on Thacher Island off Cape Ann in 1861 replaced two colonial lights dating from 1771. Placed on a north-south axis 900 ft (274 m) apart, the two towers allowed sailors to orient themselves by the alignment of the lights. The towers were built of granite blocks from New Hampshire, which was considered more suitable than local stone. Each of the Fresnel lenses was 12 ft (3.5 m) tall and weighed more than 3 tons. Illumination was initially by whale oil lamps, later changed to kerosene, and finally electricity. The northern light was withdrawn from service in 1932 and in 1980 the southern light changed to automatic operation.

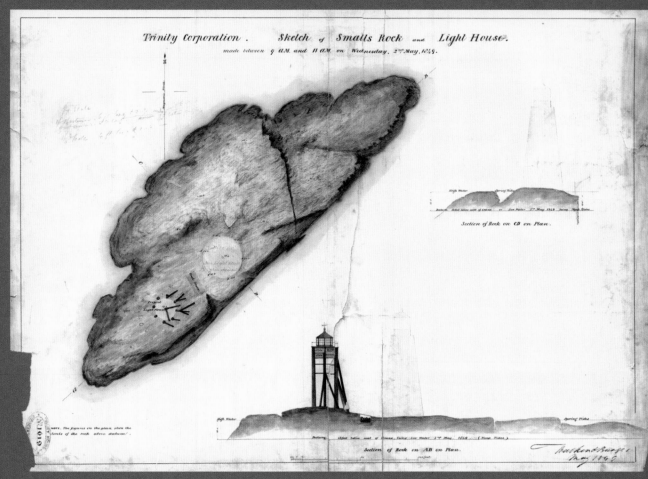

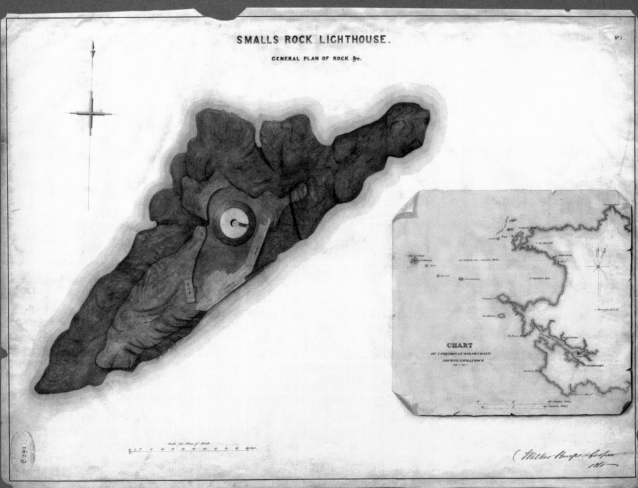

Lying in the Irish Sea, 20 miles (32 km) off the coast of Pembrokeshire, the Smalls Rocks were a major hazard to shipping. The first lighthouse built there, erected by Henry Whiteside in 1776, was a wooden structure on stilts (opposite, top). Work on replacing this ungainly but successful light with a modern stone lighthouse began in 1856. It was built by James Douglass as on-site engineer to a design by James Walker. Its innovations included a stepped, rather than smooth, base to the tower and the luxury of a built-in toilet. The Smalls lighthouse is still in service.

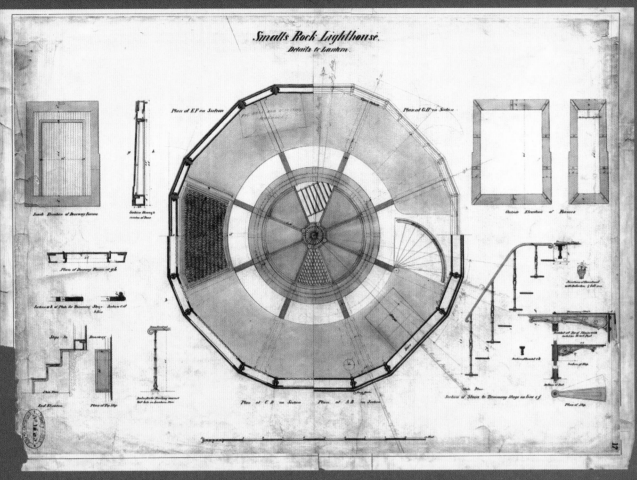

1862 SÖDERSKÄR
PORVOO ARCH. | FINLAND

DESIGNED BY **ALBERT EDELFELT AND ERNST LOHRMANN** | TOWER: **OCTAGONAL STONE AND BRICK** | HEIGHT: **131 FT (40 M)** | LIGHT: **UNKNOWN**

PROJEKT TILL EN FYRBÅK

Söderskär lighthouse stands on Mattlandet island in the Gulf of Finland, some 18 miles (30 km) from Helsinki. When the light was built, Finland was part of the Russian Empire. Established in response to a rise in Baltic sea traffic, the lighthouse was originally intended to be a stone tower, but granite was in short supply and eventually only the base of the tower, up to 26 ft (8 m) in height, was made of stone, the remainder built of brick. The barrack put up to house the construction workers became the lighthouse keeper's cottage. The light continued in operation until 1989.

PÅ SÖDERSKÄR I BORGÅ SOCKEN

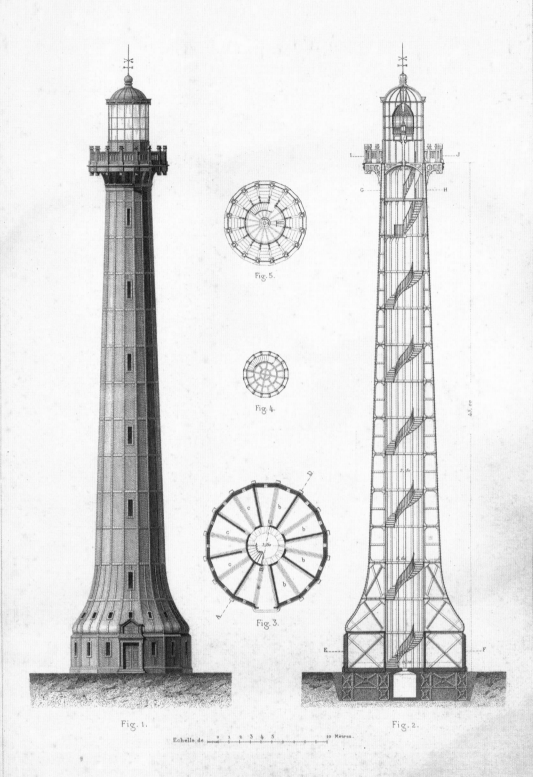

Fig. 5.

Fig. 4.

Fig. 3.

Fig. 1.

Echelle de   0 1 2 3 4 5   10 Mètres.

Fig. 2.

S^{us} Bertin del.

J. Sulpis sc.

PHARE DE LA NOUVELLE CALÉDONIE.

In 1859, the French decided that a lighthouse was needed to mark a safe passage through the reef around Grande Terre, the main island of their Pacific colony of New Caledonia. Consisting of an internal iron structure clad in iron panels, the lighthouse was built at the Rigolet works in Paris in 1862.

After standing as a Parisian landmark for two years, in 1864 it was disassembled and transported down the Seine to Le Havre by barge. From there, the parts were shipped to New Caledonia, where the lighthouse was re-erected at its current site. It is one of the world's tallest iron towers.

1867 BIG SABLE
MICHIGAN | USA

CHIEF ENGINEER: **COLONEL ORLANDO M. POE**
TOWER: **CIRCULAR BRICK** | HEIGHT: **112 FT (34 M)**
LIGHT: **THIRD-ORDER FRESNEL LENS**

'E'

TOWER

FOR

BIG SABLE. LAKE SUPERIOR

Scale ¼ in to 1 f!

PLAN of MAIN DECK and PARAPIT

PLAN of LAST LANDING

FIRST LANDING

GROUND PLAN

ELEVATION

SECTION.

The lighthouse built at Big Sable Point on the eastern shore of Lake Michigan formed part of a general drive to improve the safety of navigation on the Great Lakes. The structure consists of a tapering brick tower standing on stone foundations that reach more than 6 ft (1.8 m) under ground. A keeper's house was linked to the lighthouse by a covered passage. The lighthouse's yellow-hued Milwaukee Cream City bricks began to crumble over time and, as a result, in 1900 the building was enclosed in cylindrical metal siding. In recent years, it has been the object of a notable conservation effort.

1867 TYBEE
GEORGIA | USA

DESIGNED BY **JOHN MULLRYNE** IN **1773** | TOWER:
OCTAGONAL BRICK | HEIGHT: **154 FT (47 M)** IN **1867**
LIGHT: **FIRST-ORDER FRESNEL LENS**

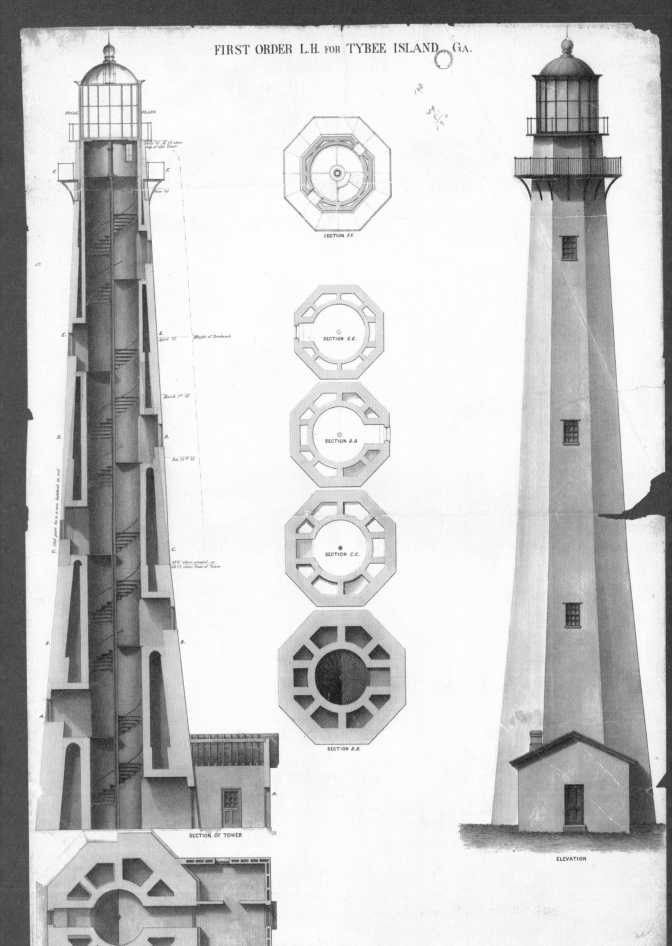

FIRST ORDER L.H. FOR TYBEE ISLAND, GA.

SECTION F.F.

SECTION E.E.

SECTION D.D.

SECTION C.C.

SECTION B.B.

SECTION OF TOWER

SECTIONAL PLAN A.A.

ELEVATION

Scale. 3/16 Inch = 1 Foot
Time of Lighting Oct. 1st 1867

DESIGN FOR A LIGHTHOUSE TOWER
ON THE ISLAND OF SOMBRERO IN THE WEST INDIES
TO ACCOMPANY Mr PARKES' REPORT TO THE BOARD OF TRADE
DATED 19th DECEMBER 1866

ELEVATION

SECTION

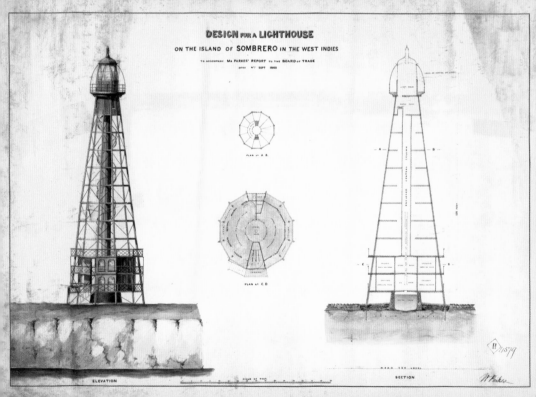

DESIGN FOR A LIGHTHOUSE
ON THE ISLAND OF SOMBRERO IN THE WEST INDIES
TO ACCOMPANY Mr PARKES' REPORT TO THE BOARD OF TRADE
DATED 4th SEPT 1865

ELEVATION

SECTION

OPPOSITE The first functioning lighthouse on Tybee Island was a 100-ft (30-m) tower built in 1773. This structure was severely damaged in the Civil War. The bottom 60 ft (18 m) of the tower were retained when the lighthouse was rebuilt in 1866–67. An iron spiral staircase replaced wooden stairs.

ABOVE These designs were made for a lighthouse on Sombrero Island in the Caribbean. In 1868, an iron skeletal structure built by Thames Ironworks and Shipbuilding Co. was erected on Sombrero. It differed from the design above in having no integrated keeper's accommodation. The light served until 1962.

1868 CAPE CANAVERAL
FLORIDA | USA

DESIGNER **WILLIAM F. SMITH** | TOWER:
CIRCULAR IRON AND BRICK | HEIGHT: **151 FT**
(46 M) | LIGHT: **FIRST-ORDER FRESNEL LENS**

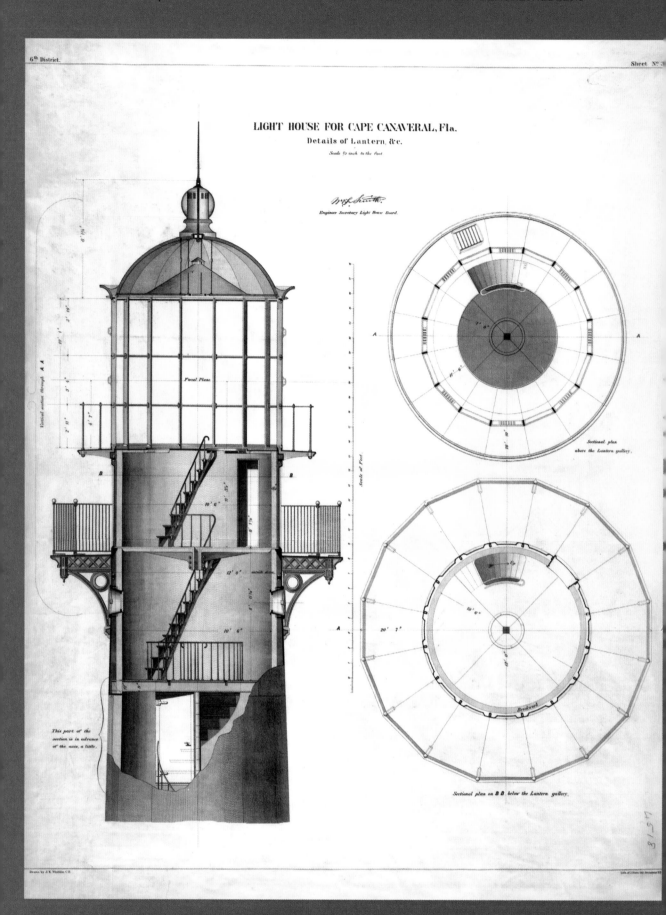

LIGHT HOUSE FOR CAPE CANAVERAL, Fla.

Details of Lantern, &c.

Scale ½ inch to the Foot

Engineer Secretary Light House Board.

The first lighthouse at Cape Canaveral was a 65-ft
(20-m) brick tower built in 1848. Its inadequacy was
soon acknowledged. Work on a new light began in 1860
but was delayed by the Civil War. The structure was made
of cast-iron plates bolted together and lined on the inside
with bricks. The original access was by an external staircase.
To escape coastal erosion, in 1893–94 the whole building was
shifted a mile inland, the metal plates hauled by mules along
an improvised railway. A witness to many rocket launches,
the lighthouse is now within Cape Canaveral Air Force Station.

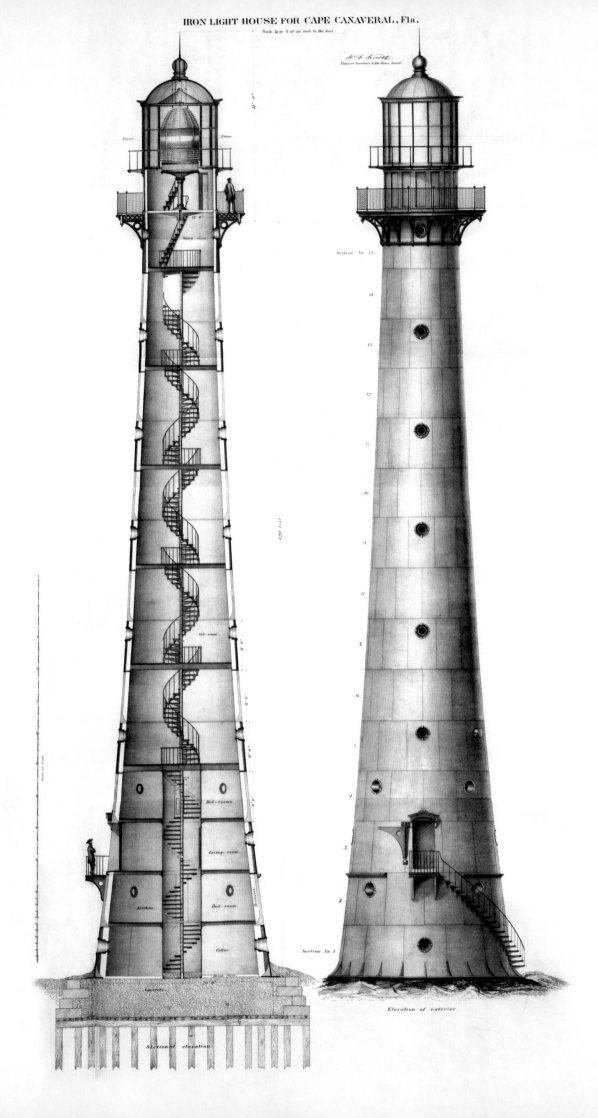

Sectional elevation.

Elevation of exterior.

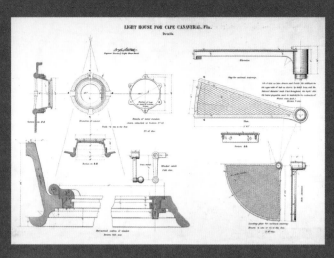

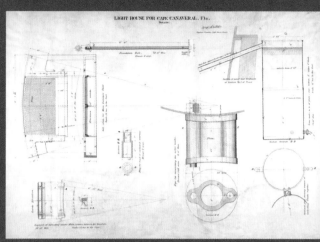

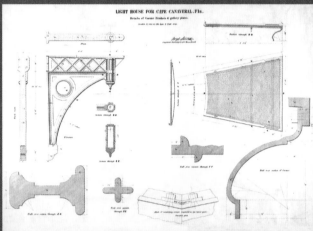

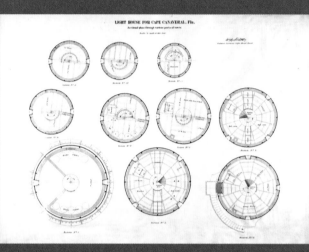

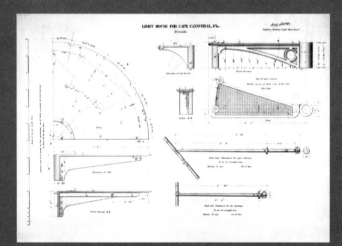

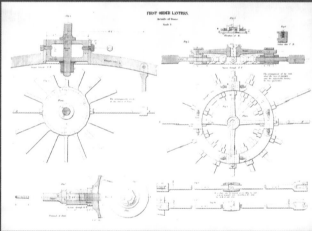

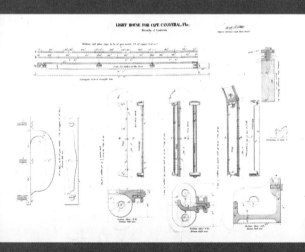

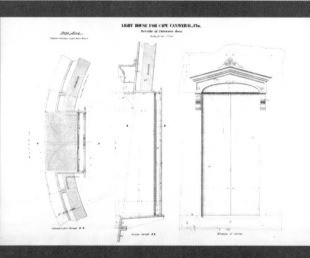

These plans show internal details of the Cape Canaveral lighthouse built in 1868. Initially the assistant keepers lived inside the building, which included two bedrooms, a living room, and a kitchen on the bottom three floors. Only the head keeper enjoyed the privilege of a house apart. However, the heat inside the iron-clad tower was so unbearably uncomfortable that all the keepers eventually had to be found external accommodation. The cylindrical tower tapers, as can be seen in the shrinking of the circular floor plans from the bottom to the top story (above right, second from top).

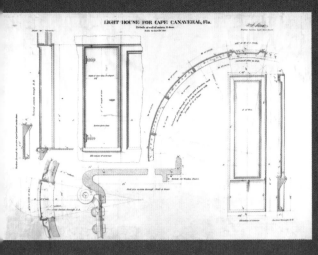

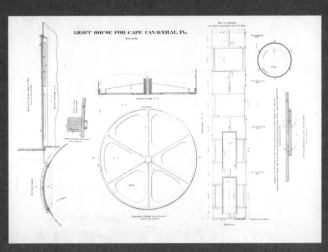

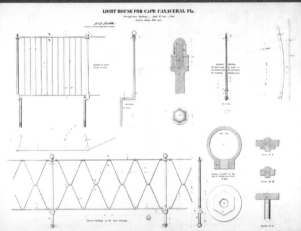

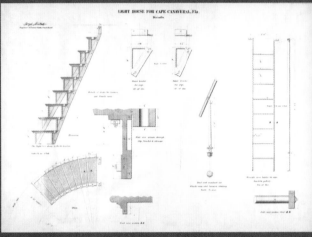

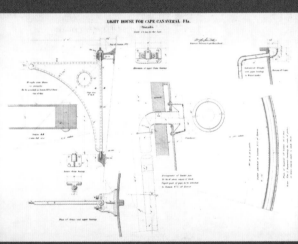

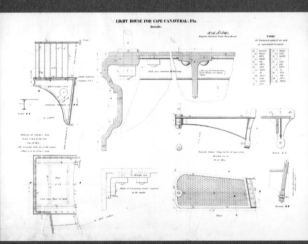

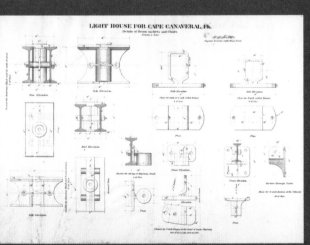

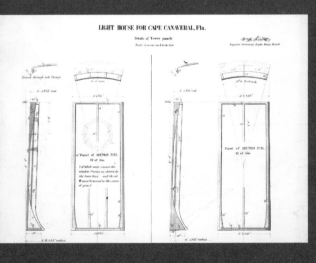

370 WOLF ROCK
CORNWALL | ENGLAND

DESIGNED BY **JAMES WALKER** | TOWER: **CIRCULAR STONE ON CONCRETE BASE** | HEIGHT: **135 FT (41 M)** | LIGHT: **CHANCE FOURTH-ORDER CATADIOPTRIC LENS**

SECTION OF A STONE LIGHT HOUSE DESIGNED FOR THE WOLF ROCK

By Robert Stevenson Esq.r Civil Engineer after being Surveyed by him according to the

ORDERS OF THE ADMIRALTY IN 1823.

DESIGN FOR A COLUMNAL BRONZE LIGHT HOUSE

PROPOSED TO BE ERECTED ON THE WOLF ROCK THE SAME HEIGHT AS THE EDYSTONE LIGHT-HOUSE

By Sam.l Brown Commander R.N.

FIG. 1.

FIG. 1.

It was long thought impossible to build a lighthouse on this exposed rock between Land's End and the Scilly Isles. The proposed 1823 design (above), by Robert Stevenson, was never built. James Walker's lighthouse, for which plans

difficulty between 1861 and 1869, with William Douglass serving as on-site engineer. Douglass described the Chance Brothers lens (bottom right) as "the most perfect for the purpose that has yet been constructed." The lighthouse

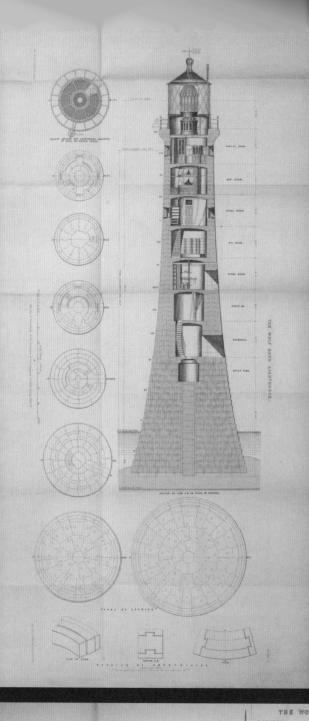

THE WOLF ROCK LIGHTHOUSE.

SECTION ON LINE A B ON PLAN OF COURSES.

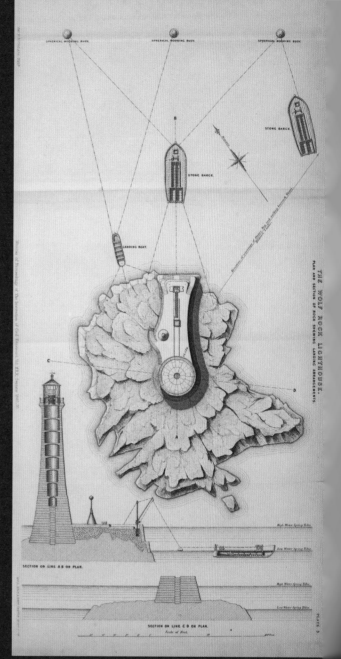

THE WOLF ROCK LIGHTHOUSE.

PLAN AND SECTION OF ROCK SHEWING LANDING ARRANGEMENTS.

SECTION ON LINE A B ON PLAN.

SECTION ON LINE C D ON PLAN.

PLATE 3.

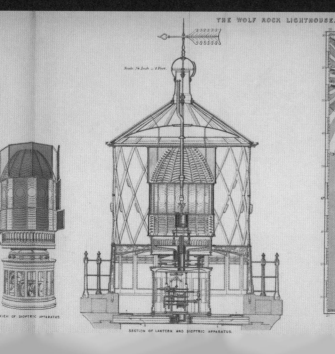

THE WOLF ROCK LIGHTHOUSE.

Scale ¾ Inch = 1 Foot.

VIEW OF DIOPTRIC APPARATUS.

SECTION OF LANTERN AND DIOPTRIC APPARATUS.

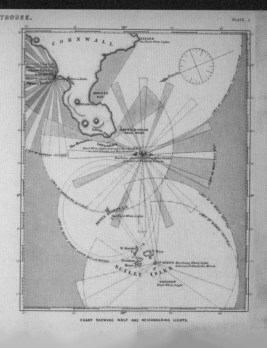

PLATE 2.

CHART SHEWING WOLF AND NEIGHBOURING LIGHTS.

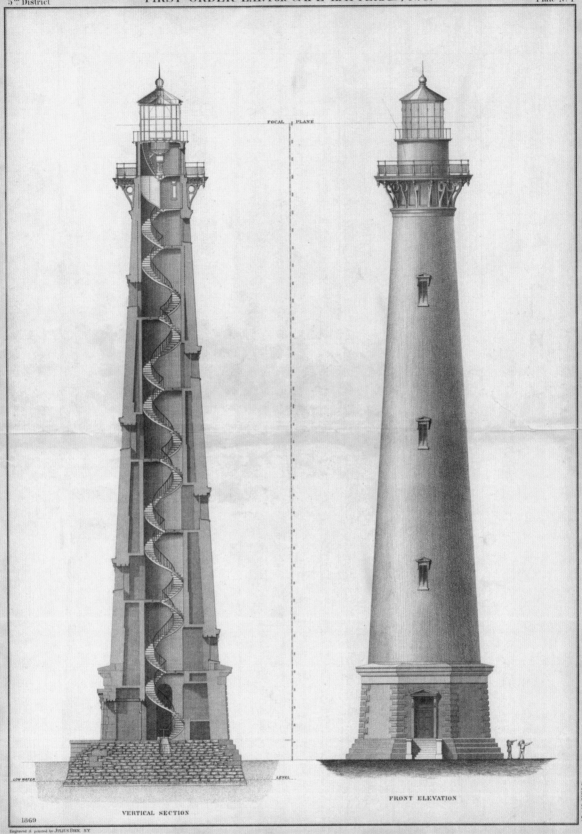

FOCAL PLANE

LOW WATER   LEVEL

VERTICAL SECTION

FRONT ELEVATION

1869

Engraved & printed by JULIUS BIEN. N.Y.

Plate Nº 1.

The shifting sandbars of the Diamond Shoals off Cape Hatteras took such a toll of shipping that they became known as "the Graveyard of the Atlantic." The first lighthouse at Cape Hatteras, built in 1802, suffered damage in the Civil War, and after the war's end it was decided to replace rather than repair it. The new lighthouse had a lofty conical brick tower mounted on an octagonal granite base. The structure survived hurricane and earthquake, but by 1935 was seriously threatened by coastal erosion. In 1999, the lighthouse was finally relocated a half-mile inland.

1872 **SAINT SIMONS GEORGIA | USA**

DESIGNED BY **CHARLES B. CLUSKEY**
TOWER: **CIRCULAR BRICK** | HEIGHT: **104 FT**
(32 M) | LIGHT: **THIRD-ORDER FRESNEL LENS**

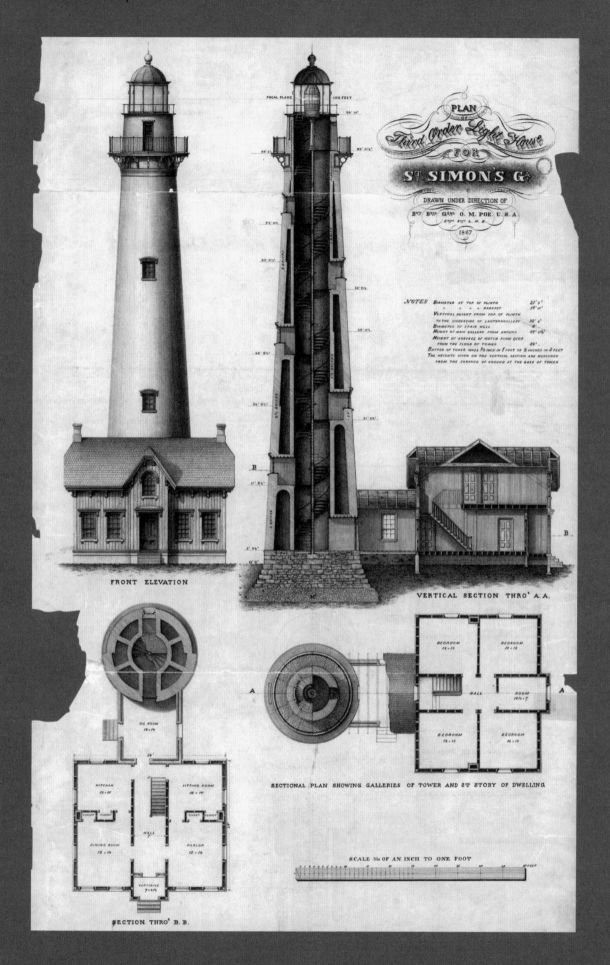

Saint Simons is a barrier island on the Georgia coast. The first lighthouse built there in 1810 was destroyed by withdrawing Confederate troops during the Civil War. Work on the current lighthouse was initiated in 1869 but encountered delays as a disease took its toll on those engaged in the project. The light was eventually lit for the first time in September 1872. Inside the tower the spiral staircase has 129 steps. The two-story keeper's dwelling attached to the light tower is now used as a museum.

1872 DUBH ARTACH
HEBRIDES | SCOTLAND

DESIGNED BY **THOMAS STEVENSON AND DAVID STEVENSON** | TOWER: **CIRCULAR STONE**
HEIGHT: **145 FT (44 M)** | LIGHT: **FRESNEL LENS**

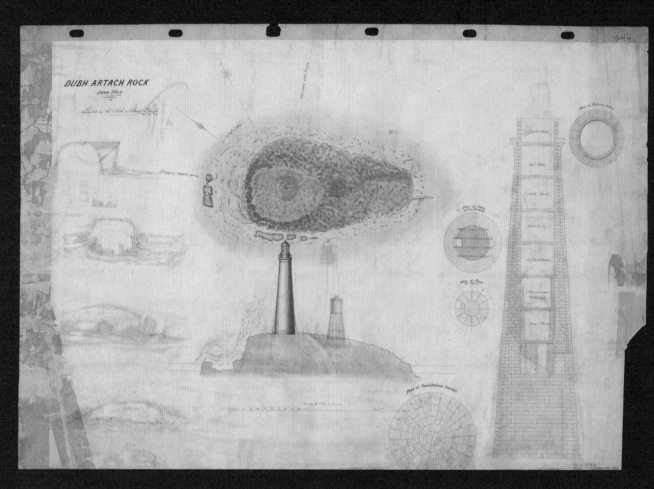

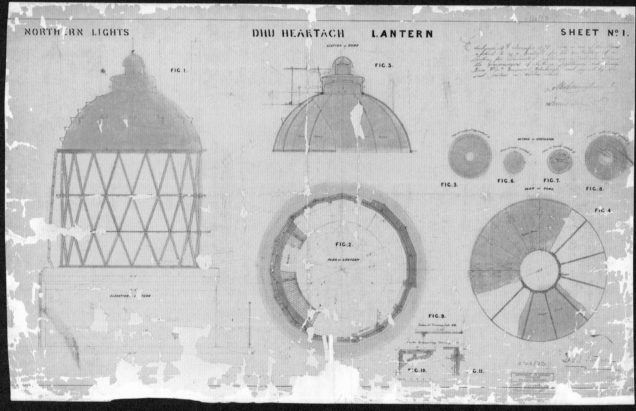

Dubh Artach is a basalt rock off the west coast of Scotland, 14 miles (22 km) from the nearest island and exposed to the full force of the Atlantic Ocean. Thomas Stevenson, aided by his brother David, began work on the lighthouse in 1866, but conditions were so challenging that the first stone was not laid until 1869. During construction, the workers were housed in an iron stilted barrack, visible alongside the lighthouse in the drawing above. The light eventually entered service in November 1872, but the tower as shown in these plans is not exactly as it was built.

1873 SAND ISLAND
ALABAMA | USA

CHIEF ENGINEER: **MAJOR GEORGE H. ELLIOT**
TOWER: **CIRCULAR STONE** | HEIGHT: **132 FT**
(40 M) | LIGHT: **SECOND-ORDER FRESNEL LENS**

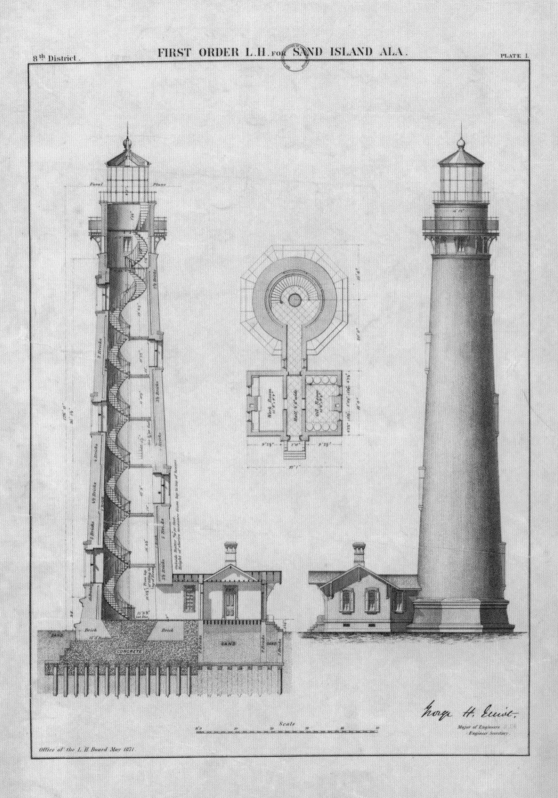

This 1873 lighthouse was the third built on Sand Island at the mouth of Mobile Bay. The first was erected in 1838. The second, a fine 150-ft (45-m) brick tower, stood for only five years before, like many Southern lights, it was destroyed in the Civil War in 1863. The third light was built, with its attached keeper's dwelling, between 1871 and 1873. A struggle against erosion began soon afterward. By 1900, it already seemed unlikely that the lighthouse could be saved as the island shrank, but continued building of sea defenses has kept the tower standing into the 21st century.

IRON LIGHT HOUSE for S.W. PASS, La.

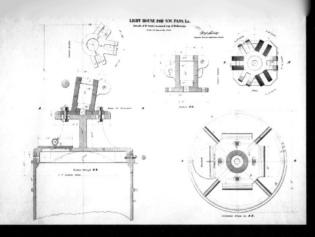

LIGHT HOUSE FOR S.W. PASS, La.
Details of 16" Service Sockets & Cap of Hollow pipe.

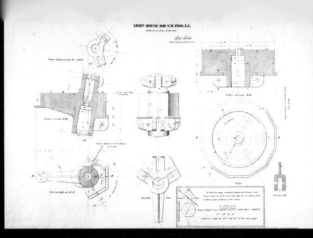

LIGHT HOUSE FOR S.W. PASS, La.

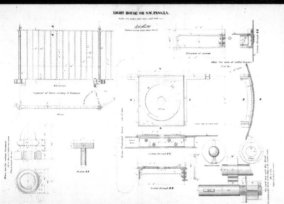

LIGHT HOUSE OR S.W. PASS, La.

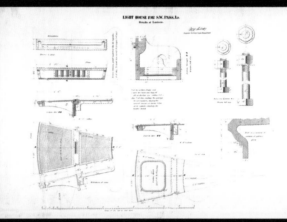

LIGHT HOUSE FOR S.W. PASS, La.
Details of Lantern.

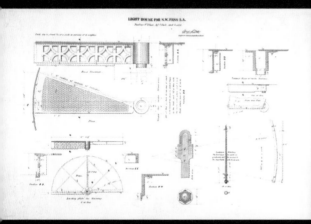

LIGHT HOUSE FOR S.W. PASS, La.

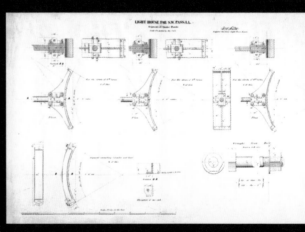

LIGHT HOUSE FOR S.W. PASS, La.

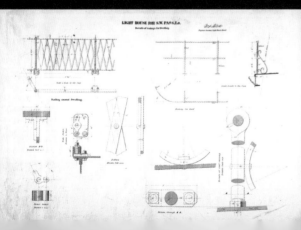

LIGHT HOUSE FOR S.W. PASS, La.

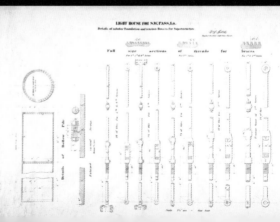

LIGHT HOUSE FOR S.W. PASS, La.
Details of tubular Foundation and Screw Braces for Superstructure.

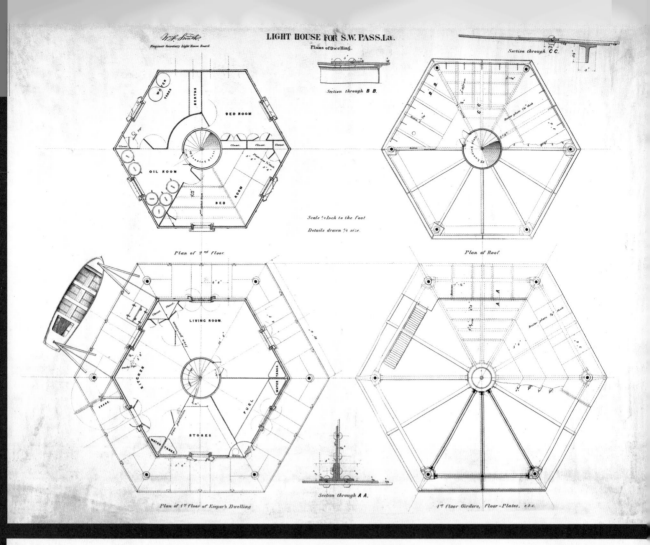

LIGHT HOUSE FOR S.W. PASS.La.

Plans of Dwelling.

Section through B B.

Section through C C.

Scale ¼ Inch to the Foot

Details drawn ¼ size.

Plan of 2nd Floor.

Plan of Roof.

Plan of 1st Floor of Keeper's Dwelling

Section through A A.

1st Floor Girders, Floor-Plates, &c.

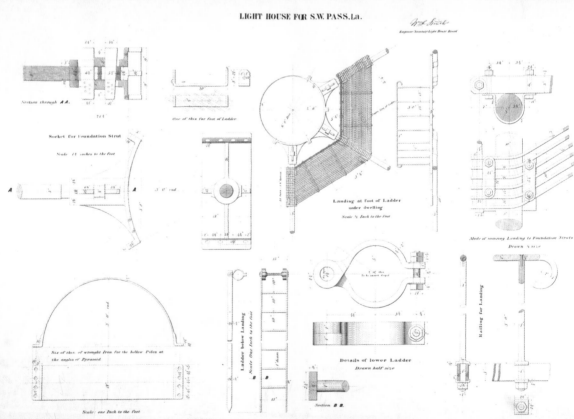

LIGHT HOUSE FOR S.W. PASS.La.

Section through A A.

Socket for Foundation Strut

Scale 1½ inches to the foot

One of these for Foot of Ladder

Landing at foot of Ladder
under dwelling

Scale ½ Inch to the Foot

Mode of securing Landing to Foundation Struts

Drawn ½ size

Size of this of wrought Iron for the hollow Piles at
the angles of Pyramid.

Scale one Inch to the foot

Ladder below Landing

Scale One Inch to the Foot

Section B B.

Details of lower Ladder

Drawn half size

Railing for Landing

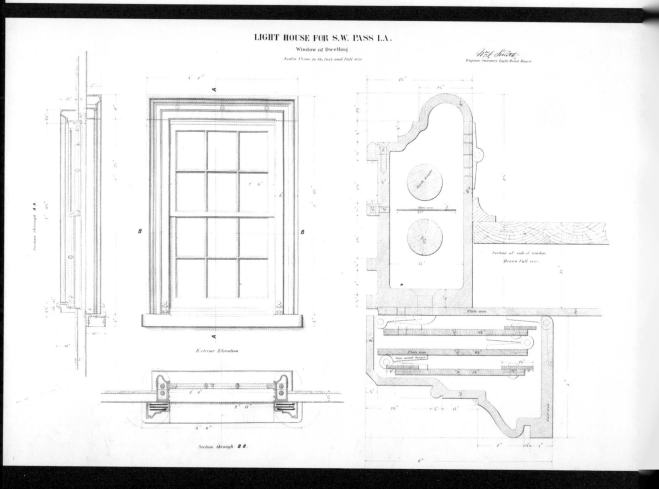

CARLINGFORD LOUGH
NORTHERN IRELAND

DESIGNER **UNKNOWN** | TOWER: **IRON SKELETAL**
HEIGHT: FRONT LIGHT **28 FT (8 M)**, REAR LIGHT
45 FT (14 M) | LIGHT: **OIL LAMPS**

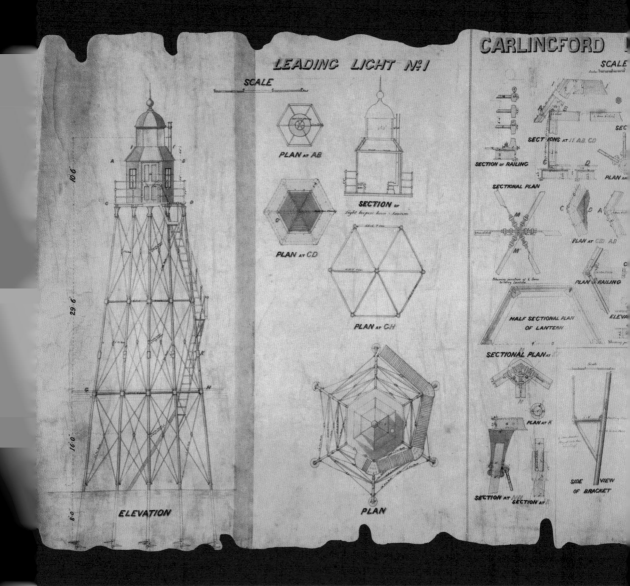

LEADING LIGHT Nº 1

CARLINGFORD

PLAN AT AB

PLAN AT CD

SECTION OF
light keeper's house lantern

PLAN AT GH

ELEVATION

PLAN

SECTIONS AT H AB. CD

SECTION OF RAILING

SECTIONAL PLAN

PLAN AT CD. AB

PLAN OF RAILING

HALF SECTIONAL PLAN
OF LANTERN

SECTIONAL PLAN AT

PLAN AT K

SIDE VIEW
OF BRACKET

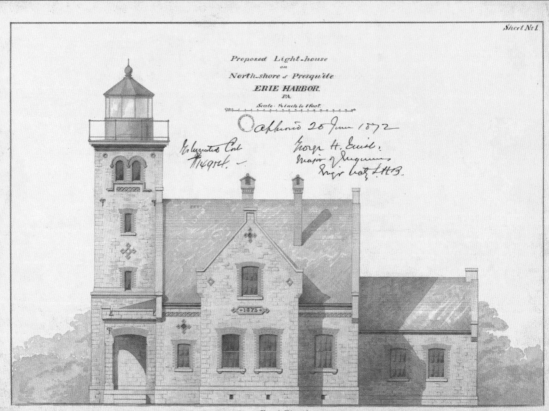

Sheet Nº 1

Proposed Light-house
on
North-shore of Presqu'ile
ERIE HARBOR.
PA.
Scale ¼ inch to 1 foot

Approved 26 June 1872

George H. Emick.
Major of Engineers

Front Elevation.
(facing North)

1873 PRESQUE ISLE
PENNSYLVANIA | USA

DESIGNER **UNKNOWN** | TOWER: **SQUARE BRICK**
ORIGINAL HEIGHT: **40 FT (12 M)** | LIGHT: **FOURTH**
ORDER FRESNEL LENS

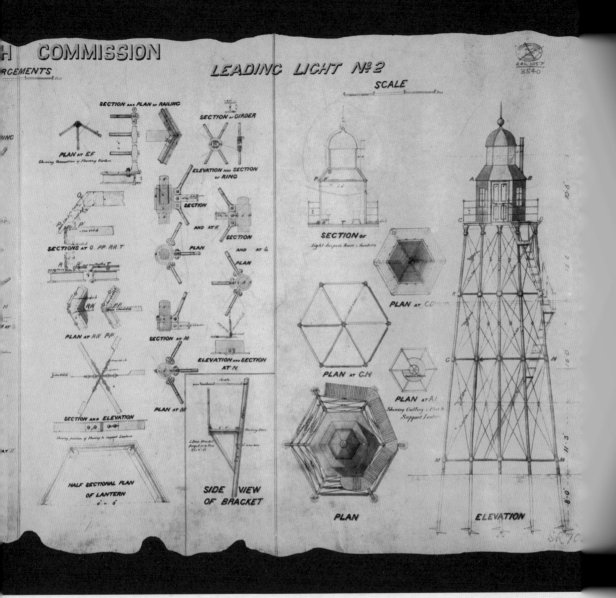

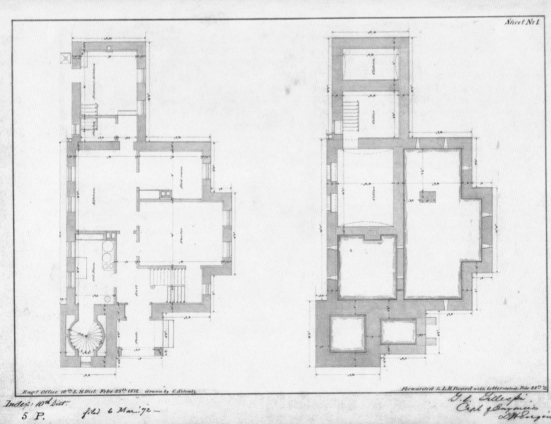

CHAPTER 4.

KEEPERS

OF THE LIGHT.

SPLENDORS AND MISERIES OF THE

LIGHTHOUSE CREWS.

Lighthouse keepers were heroes of the Victorian era, celebrated for their humble dutiful devotion to a humanitarian task, the hermit-like simplicity and solitude of their lives. Refined urbanites, tired of the complexities of city living, romanticized the keepers' nightly vigil amid the wind and waves, their meditative contemplation of nature interrupted by a seabird striking the glass of the lantern, or an occasional dramatic rescue of shipwrecked mariners. This pleasing picture did not come close to the reality of a hard and monotonous way of life. As the black sheep of a well-known Scottish family of lighthouse engineers, Robert Louis Stevenson knew more about the actual lives of lighthouse keepers than other Victorian poets. Refusing the sentimentalizing trend of his age, in his poem "The Light-Keeper" (1870) he described a man "Who gives up all that is lovely in living/For the means to live/...Sitting, patient and stolid,/Martyr to a salary." Stevenson could see lighthouse keeping for what it was: a steady but demanding job, clung to as the source of a reliable income in a tough world that offered no easy options.

In the early days of lighthouses, employment as a keeper was casual in the extreme. When a permanent light was installed on the uninhabited Isle of May in Scotland in 1636, a certain George Anderson was taken on to maintain the coal fire in return for £7 a year and extensive fishing rights. Anderson apparently took his fishing very seriously, with the consequence that the light frequently went unlit. Such an easygoing approach to illumination obviously constituted a serious danger to shipping. Over time, lighthouse keeping of necessity became a strictly regulated occupation. The *Instructions for the Lightkeepers of the Northern Lighthouses*, formulated by the Stevensons two centuries later, opened with the absolute order: "The lamps shall be kept burning bright and clear every night from sunset to sunrise...." A whole way of life was built around this simple imperative.

Since discipline and order were essential characteristics of a good keeper, there was a tendency to regard lighthouse keeping as a suitable job for men from a military or naval background. In France, former sailors and war veterans made up by far the majority of the workforce in a highly organized, bureaucratized 19th-century lighthouse service. In the United States, Joshua Strout might be considered a "typical" keeper, placed in charge of the Portland Head light (1791)

OPPOSITE

Top left: A man is winched up to the base of the lighthouse at Wolf Rock, off Lands End, during a landing in rough seas.

Top right: A figure looks out from the balcony surrounding the light room at Bell Rock.

Center left: Two keepers fill oil-butts with fuel at St. Catherine's light on the southernmost tip of the Isle of Wight.

Center: 19th-century illustration of a keeper standing on the balcony of his lighthouse, ready to catch birds attracted by the light.

Center right: Ida Lewis, keeper of Lime Rock, shown on the cover of a 1869 set of sheet music for a "Rescue Polka Mazurka" dedicated to her.

Bottom left: A keeper watches the approach of a supply vessel from the raised doorway of Skerryvore lighthouse.

Bottom right: Raising the flag, used for signaling, on the protruding platform at the top of Winstanley's second Eddystone.

ABOVE

Fig. 1.— A keeper at Kõpu lighthouse, Estonia, mounts the 119 steps in the tower.

in Maine in 1869 when he was forced to retire from his career as a merchant sea captain after a bad fall from a mast. But many factors played a part in selecting keepers in the United States, including political connections. Up to the 1880s, keepers' jobs formed part of the broad network of US political patronage that might see competent employees ejected from their posts at a change of administration to make way for less suitable but better connected replacements. In Britain, the emphasis was on selection for good character. When Robert Stevenson (1772-1850) had completed the construction of Bell Rock lighthouse in 1810, he chose two keepers: one an ex-naval sailor "possessed of the strictest notions of duty and habits of regularity" and the other a man with "one of the most happy and contented dispositions imaginable." The thinking was clear and shrewd: in a rock lighthouse, neither an undisciplined nor a gloomy temperament could be tolerated.

The overwhelming majority of lighthouse keepers were male. In a lighthouse on shore or on an islet with enough space for accommodation alongside the light, it was usually assumed that the keeper would exercise his duties with the aid of a wife and children. In the absence of the keeper, his wife would take responsibility for the light, just as in the absence of a farmer his wife would run the farm. Family members might be recognized officially and paid as assistant keepers. Although the position was never in principle heritable, sometimes on the death or retirement of the primary keeper a family member was allowed to continue the work. When Strout retired in 1904, after thirty-five years as keeper of the Portland Head lighthouse, his son Joseph – already working as assistant – succeeded to the post.

For a handful of families, lighthouse keeping became a tradition maintained through generations. Thus, members of the Garrity family in the United States provided keepers for various lights on Lake Huron from the 1860s through to the 1930s, and scions of the remarkable Knott family in England served as keepers for the original South Foreland lighthouse and other lights, from the appointment of William Knott in 1730 to the retirement of his great-great-grandson Henry Thomas Knott in 1908. It was through family succession that a certain number of women came to take charge of lighthouses in the United States. It is reckoned that some thirty widows had succeeded their husbands as keepers by

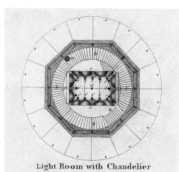

Light Room with Chandelier   2.

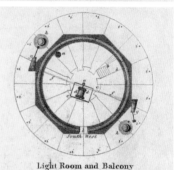

Light Room and Balcony   3.

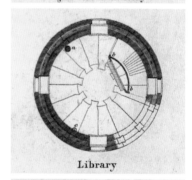

Library   4.

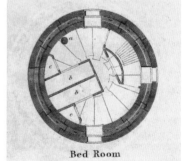

Bed Room   5.

Fig. 2.— The lantern at Bell Rock, the chandelier circled by a walkway for tending the wicks.

Fig. 3.— The Bell Rock light room with its outer balcony 98 feet (30 m) above the foundations.

Fig. 4.— The library, immediately below the light room, housed visitors as well as books.

Fig. 5.— The keepers' bedroom with two tiers of bunks side by side.

Fig. 6.— The kitchen on the third floor with a coal-fired range and a pump to bring up water.

Fig. 7.— Oil was stored on the second floor.

Fig. 8.— The storeroom housed water tanks as well as provisions.

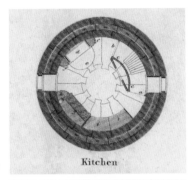

6.

Kitchen

7.

Oil Store Room

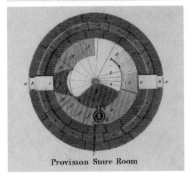

8.

Provision Store Room

the 1850s. The tradition continued into the 20th century, when Margaret Norvell, for example, took the place of her deceased husband as a keeper in Louisiana and served in that role until her retirement in 1932.

The model of the family-run lighthouse could not be applied to lights built on barren rocks or rising straight out of the sea. These isolated towers became an exclusively male preserve, known in the United States as "stag lights." They were in principle operable by two men working shifts, but it was usual to have a crew of three in the lighthouse at all times. A dramatic story was circulated in support of this level of staffing. Apparently, in the early days of British rock lighthouses there were only two keepers. Whether at Smeaton's Eddystone in Plymouth or the Smalls lighthouse in Wales or the Longships lighthouse off Land's End - the same story is told of all three with minor variations - one of the keepers died during a period of bad weather that cut off the station from the land. The other keeper did not dump the dead body into the sea because he feared an accusation of murder. After four weeks, when the storm subsided and relief arrived, the unfortunate man was discovered half-mad, with the lighthouse rendered uninhabitable by the smell of the putrefying corpse. Even in the absence of such melodrama, it was evident that a third keeper was needed if the light was to be maintained consistently in case of sickness or death. And a third keeper on station implied a team of four for each rock lighthouse, since the men would have to be given shore leave in rotation; an unrelieved period of two months or so immured in a tower in the ocean was considered as much as the human psyche could bear.

Living conditions in an offshore tower light were spartan. Typically, there would be three rooms - a kitchen, living room, and bedroom - each occupying a floor, sandwiched between storage rooms below and the service room and lantern above. All the rooms were circular, about 12 feet (3.6 m) in diameter, with the weight tube in the middle. Consequently, the men's bunks had to be curved to fit the shape of the bedroom walls. The whole interior of the tower was dark because of the extreme thickness of the walls and the smallness of the few windows. The only escape from this confinement was up onto the narrow gallery outside the lantern - not suitable for acrophobes, as it stood more than 98 feet (30 m) above the sea - or down onto whatever exiguous extent of rock or concrete might be accessible at the foot of the tower at low tide and in fair weather. Naturally, the lantern provided magnificent sea views that were appreciated by those keepers whose taste for marine beauty was not sated by excess. Isolation seems the most obvious characteristic of lighthouses. It is easy to understand why the Stannard Rock light (1883) on Lake Superior, more than 20 miles (32 km) from land, came to be dubbed the "loneliest place in the world." But for many keepers on rock lights, the dominant experience was rather of enforced proximity to their fellow man, and the sharing of a confined space with the rest of the crew necessarily exacerbated any personal tensions.

The keepers of lights on land led an existence not radically different from that of many other rural or coastal dwellers, especially if their lighthouse was close to a village or port. Commonly, the keeper and his family would augment their diet with a little fishing or a smallholding with a few chickens, a cow, or a pig. Vacations were unknown, and the routine of tending the light was sustained without a break seven days a week for years on end. Keeper families on small islands faced the added difficulties of being linked to the rest of the world only by the treacherous sea. They were dependent on small boats for supplies of food and fuel as well as for access to doctors, churches, and schools. Adverse weather could sever this link to civilization for weeks at a time. At least, unlike the inhabitants of the stag towers, they were usually able to go outside the buildings to fish or garden. It was known for the smaller children to be sent out to play tethered to a rope, to prevent them from falling into the sea.

It is not surprising, given the sheer difficulty of landing at many sites, that offshore lighthouses were often cut off for long periods, with crew in tower lights unrelieved well beyond the end of their allotted two-month tour of duty. David Stevenson (1815-86), who had plentiful experience in the matter, wrote with studied understatement: "The process of landing amid surf and breakers on tide-covered reefs or rock-bound coasts...is not the most agreeable duty connected with the service." In anything but the calmest of weather, crew ferried to the lighthouse were likely to arrive seasick and shaken by the journey. They would then have to stand in the pitching boat and leap as it reached the top of an upward swing, only to land awkwardly and often painfully on rock or concrete. Alternatively, there might be a precarious

Fig. 9.— Cutaway of Bell Rock lighthouse, showing how supplies were brought up the external ladder.
Fig. 10.— Plan of the Scottish Inchkeith lighthouse (1804), showing keepers' quarters.
Fig. 11.— A keeper leaving a lighthouse is winched precariously down to a small boat.

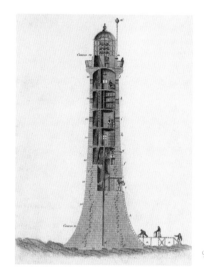

9.

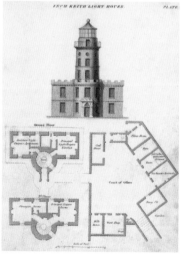

10.

11.

winch system to wind them from the boat to the foot of the lighthouse suspended from a line in a bosun's chair. From the base of one of the exposed rock towers, they might then have to climb some 30 feet (9 m) up a vertical set of iron rungs fixed into the tower wall before reaching the heavy metal entrance door. Being a keeper on a rock lighthouse was not an occupation for the unfit or the faint-hearted.

The general duties of a keeper, as set out in the regulations governing the service in different countries, were predominantly domestic and methodical. A keeper's most demanding activity was cleaning. According to the instructions to Scottish lighthouse keepers, for example, it was their daily duty to "polish or otherwise cleanse the Reflectors or Refractors till they are brought into a proper state of brilliancy…thoroughly cleanse the Lamps and carefully dust the Chandelier…cleanse the glass of the Lantern, lamp-glasses, copper and brasswork and utensils, the walls, floors, and balcony of the Light-room, and the apparatus and machinery therewith connected; together with the Tower stair, passage, doors and windows, from the Light-room to the Oil cellar." It is hardly surprising that one US keeper described "brasswork" as "the bane of a lighthouse keeper's life." These rules were enforced by much-feared inspectors who descended on the lighthouses unannounced. They examined every nook and cranny for a trace of dust or a finger mark, and threatened dismissal for an unmade bed or an unkempt personal appearance (the Scottish instructions required keepers to be "cleanly in their persons and linens, and orderly in their families"). The inspectors would also take careful note of stores of fuel and other supplies, to check no wastage or purloining was taking place, and would verify that logbook entries were in order. Maintaining a detailed log was a duty of the lighthouse keeper modeled on naval practice. He had to record the readings from a barometer, thermometer, and rain gauge, the direction and strength of the wind, and the identity of any passing ships. Sometimes keepers expanded their entries to include observations of nature, irrelevant details of their daily lives, or general philosophical reflections.

The routines involved in "tending the light" varied according to the light source and technology. Oil lamps required careful attention, with wicks trimmed to burn evenly and the supply of fuel to the wicks regulated. The clockwork mechanism that made non-fixed lights rotate had to be

12.

13.

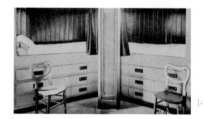
14.

Fig. 12.— Keeper in the oil room of a lighthouse, early 20th century.

Fig. 13.— Combined kitchen and living room in a lighthouse, c. 1900.

Fig. 14.— Compact sleeping accommodation for two keepers, c. 1900.

Fig. 15.— Cleaning the lantern windows in a French lighthouse in the 1930s.

Fig. 16.— A keeper fitting a new bulb for an electric light in 1946.

Fig. 17.— In the 1930s, a French lighthouse keeper takes his ease.

15.

16.

17.

wound up at regular intervals, typically every four hours. Low visibility conditions were often the most exhausting for the keepers, as they were then required to periodically ring the fog bell, fire the fog gun, or activate the siren. In principle, the keeper on shift was never supposed to leave the light room unoccupied during the hours of darkness. It was in his lonely night-time vigil, enclosed in his glass eyrie amid the howling of the wind and the roar of the waves from far below, that he came closest to the romantic image of a solitary sentinel keeping watch over the ocean.

In addition to maintaining the log, the keeper was required to record separately any shipwrecks observed from the lighthouse, with details of how they occurred. Shipwrecks provided most of the high drama in the history of lighthouses – ironically, since wrecks were, of course, what lighthouses were supposed to prevent. Positioned in isolation at some of the most notoriously dangerous places on the world's coasts, the keepers of the light would likely be first on the scene to try to save shipwrecked sailors and passengers from an awful death. This humane intervention fed the Victorian taste for sentimental melodrama and self-sacrificing idealism. Whereas lighthouse folk themselves seem to have taken a down-to-earth practical view of acts of rescue, regarding them as "all in the day's work," the general public was enthused by tales of the keepers' heroism, which became some of the most oft-repeated stories of the age.

Grace Darling was the daughter of the keeper of the Longstone light. Sited on the rocky Farne Islands off the coast of Northumberland, northeast England, Longstone lighthouse was built in 1826 to replace an antiquated coal-burning light on neighboring Brownsman Island. The keeper from the Brownsman light, William Darling, transferred to the Longstone with his family, including eleven-year-old Grace. By all accounts a quiet and conscientious young woman, she became her father's chief helper after her brothers moved away. On a rough night in September 1838, the paddle steamer *Forfarshire*, with more than sixty passengers and crew on board, lost power from its engines and was washed onto the Big Harcar Rock, about a mile from the Longstone. Most of those on board were swept away as the ship broke up, but at daybreak a terrified remnant still clung onto rocks and wreckage. Grace was first to hear their piteous cries and urged her father to launch the lighthouse's flimsy flat-bottomed boat into the raging sea. With great danger and difficulty, father and daughter rowed to the scene of the wreck. In two trips, nine survivors were rescued and brought to safety at the lighthouse. When the young woman's courageous part in the rescue became known, the Victorian public took her into their hearts. The lighthouse was besieged by artists eager to paint her portrait and also by day trippers agog to see the site of the drama. Queen Victoria contributed £50 to a public subscription for her benefit. The Duke of Northumberland appointed himself her unofficial protector. This sudden celebrity did not suit the Darling family, who did their best to continue with their regular duties. Grace's father held that the pressure of publicity contributed to the decline of his daughter's health. She died of tuberculosis in 1842, aged twenty-six. William Wordsworth, England's most renowned poet, wrote some sentimental verse in her memory, exalting "A Maiden gentle, yet, at duty's call/Firm and unflinching...."

The United States found its own favorite lighthouse daughter in Idawalley Zorada Lewis of Newport, Rhode Island. Ida was the daughter of the keeper of the light on Lime Rock in Newport Harbor, retired sea captain Hosea Lewis. As Lime Rock (1854) was a relatively tame harbor light, there were no shipwrecks to cope with, but the waters were cold and treacherous enough to provide occasions for heroism. As early as 1854, when she was only twelve years old, Ida rowed to the rescue of four people who had got into difficulties in the harbor. She is reckoned to have gone on to save the lives of at least fourteen other people during her long career at the lighthouse. It was her rescue of two soldiers, when their boat capsized in a snowstorm in March 1869, that brought nationwide fame. Lauded by the press, she was showered with medals and offers of marriage, visited by President Ulysses Grant, cited as an example of women's capacities by suffragist Susan B. Anthony, and subjected to the curiosity of hundreds of summer visitors who came to wonder at "the bravest woman in America." Ida was a rather shy person who did not much welcome attention. She concentrated on her work at the lighthouse, where she was made official keeper in 1879 after both her parents had died. Ida held the post until her own death in 1911.

Naturally, when major shipwrecks occurred there was usually little lighthouse keepers could do to mitigate the disaster. In 1856, for example, the cargo ship *Welsford*

18.

19.

20.

Fig. 18.— *Grace Darling rows to rescue survivors of the* Forfarshire *wreck.*

Fig. 19.— *Darling comforts* Forfarshire *survivors in the Longstone kitchen.*

Fig. 20.— *American hero Ida Lewis.*

Fig. 21.— *The wreck of the* Daniel Steinmann *near Sambro Island lighthouse in 1884.*

Fig. 22.— *The* Annie C. Maguire *on the rocks near Portland Head light in 1886.*

Fig. 23.— *The* Annie C. Maguire *crew rescued.*

21.

22.

23.

ran aground near the newly built Cape Race light on the southeast tip of Newfoundland. The keeper and his assistant saved four crew members by running a line down a cliff, but twenty-two others perished. In 1884, the steamship *Daniel Steinmann* sank near Sambro Island, the site of North America's oldest working lighthouse guarding the entrance to Halifax harbor, Nova Scotia. Of 130 people on board, only nine survived to be rescued by the keepers. The Strout family at Portland Head light, Maine, had better success on the night of Christmas Eve, 1886. With heavy snow falling, the British sailing barque *Annie C. Maguire* struck a rock ledge only 98 feet (30 m) from the lighthouse tower. Keeper Joshua Strout and his son Joseph put a ladder across to the ship while Joshua's wife, Mary, illuminated the scene by burning blankets soaked in kerosene. All the eighteen-strong crew of the vessel were soon safely ashore and eating Christmas chicken pie in one of the lighthouse buildings.

The unbending Scottish "Lighthouse Stevensons" would have strongly disapproved of the Strouts' humane provision of aid and succor to the crew of the *Maguire*. Writing in 1864, David Stevenson bluntly pointed out that "if the light-keepers were, in case of shipwreck, to render any personal service at all, it would necessarily take them away from the lighthouse in states of the weather when it is all-important that the light room duties should be performed with, if possible, more than ordinary assiduity...." This was an extreme view, perhaps, but it is true that the organization of lifeboat services in the course of the 19th century – such as the Royal National Lifeboat Institution in Britain in 1824 and the United States Life-Saving Service in 1878 – provided a potentially more effective response to shipwrecks. Yet it was still likely that lighthouse keepers might be first on the scene. As late as 1927, keeper Fred Kreth, at the notoriously isolated Point Reyes light (1870) in California, saved three fishermen whose boat had run onto rocks below his station. Kreth went part way down the cliff on a rope, then lowered the rope to the men trapped below. By the time the Coast Guard arrived to effect a rescue, the fishermen were safe in the lighthouse.

Unfortunately, sometimes the lighthouse keepers themselves were the people in need of saving, and salvation was not always at hand. The United States' very first keeper, George Worthylake, appointed in 1716 to run the Boston light on Little Brewster Island, was drowned in November

1718, along with his wife, daughter, and three other people, in a boat accident on his way back to the station. The young Benjamin Franklin published a poem on the sad occasion, telling how: "Quick the prow is upward borne/George in Ann's arms is thrown/Husband, wife and child together/To the chilly waves have gone." Drowning, most often when a small boat capsized, ranked high among the random occupational hazards of a keeper's life, along with falls from height, fires caused by lamp fuel, explosions when operating the fog gun, and even lightning strikes.

Stormy weather could on rare occasions turn the shelter of a lighthouse into a death trap. On October 10, 1846, the Key West light (1825) in Florida was struck by the exceptionally violent storm known to history as the Great Havana Hurricane. The keeper of the light was widow Barbara Mabrity. As the wind rose, people fleeing from Key West town came to shelter in the base of the brick lighthouse tower, where Mabrity's children were also huddled. The keeper was tending the lamp in the light room when the tower began to rock and groan menacingly. She ran screaming down the spiral staircase and exited the door as the tower collapsed. Fourteen people died, buried inside the tower, including nearly all Mabrity's family. The neighboring Sand Key light (1827) was destroyed in the same storm, killing six. With a stoicism typical of the age, Mabrity continued as keeper of the rebuilt Key West light until fired by the Union for her Confederate sympathies in 1864, at the age of eighty-two.

Allusion has already been made to the disaster that struck the first lighthouse built on Minot's Ledge off Massachusetts in 1850, its experimental iron skeleton structure supposedly immune to the battering of the waves. Its first keeper resigned after ten months, complaining that the tower reeled in a storm like a drunken man. The second keeper was a retired English sailor, John Bennett. He grumbled constantly about the evident instability of the structure, but nothing was done. In April 1851, a major storm struck the Massachusetts coast. Bennett was onshore fetching supplies, and had left the light to the care of his two assistants. In the middle of the wild night, a desperate clanging of the fog bell was heard, a futile call for help from the assistant keepers on the collapsing lighthouse. At dawn, only broken iron pilings and debris showed where the tower had stood. One assistant drowned; the other died of exposure after swimming to a nearby

24.

25.

Fig. 24.— *The remote Eilean Mor lighthouse in the Outer Hebrides.*

Fig. 25.— *The unfortunate three keepers who disappeared without trace at Eilean Mor in 1900.*

THE LIFE
OF A
LIGHTHOUSE
KEEPER IS
NOT WITHOUT
A CERTAIN
MONOTONY;
BUT...IT IS
DEVOTED
TO A HIGH
AND HOLY
SERVICE.
THERE IS
ABOUT IT
A...HEROIC
SIMPLICITY.

W.H.D. ADAMS
1870

rock. Their ghosts are said to have haunted the new stone lighthouse built at Minot's Ledge a decade later.

One of the strangest lighthouse disasters occurred at the Eilean Mòr light (1899) in the Flannan Islands, a remote outlier of the Outer Hebrides off the northwest coast of Scotland. The only inhabitants of the tiny island of Eilean Mòr were colonies of seabirds and the lighthouse crew. These numbered the usual four men, with three staffing the light at any one time while the fourth took his month's break on shore. On December 26, 1900, the service boat arrived at Eilean Mòr bringing the relief keeper back from his break. He found the lighthouse deserted. The three keepers had disappeared without trace. Entries in the lighthouse log described the emotional distress of the crew in an exceptionally fierce storm. The last entry, for December 15, read: "Storm ended, sea calm. God is over all."

The psychological pressures of a lighthouse keeper's life should not be exaggerated. Obviously, the keeper who could walk up a staircase in his family home to the top of the tower attached and, the light once lit, come back down for supper with his wife and children was not under any great pressure. The rock lights were another matter entirely, but many men found an austere satisfaction in the routines and the remoteness. Some expressed special satisfaction at the experience of the dark hours of the middle watch when, in the words of David Stevenson, "night after night, amid the roar of waves and the howl of tempest, he holds his watch in solitude." Keepers on rock lights had a lot in common with sailors: they saw their families intermittently and spent long periods in a confined space with modest discomforts. There was much grousing about food and about poor sanitary arrangements. The experience of a great storm battering the tower with almost inconceivable violence would strike a visceral terror into any heart. Frustration could mount when a keeper was due shore leave but could not be taken off because of continual bad weather. For men unsuited to the job, a lighthouse tower might come to seem like a prison. Some keepers turned to drink; some played hooky from their posts; some crews were riven by personal feuds. But the great majority of keepers worked contentedly enough for many years, finding companionship in their colleagues and taking a modest pride and satisfaction from an important job dutifully done.

1873 GREAT BASSES
BASSES REEF | SRI LANKA

DESIGNED BY **JAMES DOUGLASS** | TOWER: **CIRCULAR**
STONE ON CYLINDRICAL BASE | HEIGHT: **121 FT (37 M)**
LIGHT: **CHANCE FIRST-ORDER DIOPTRIC**

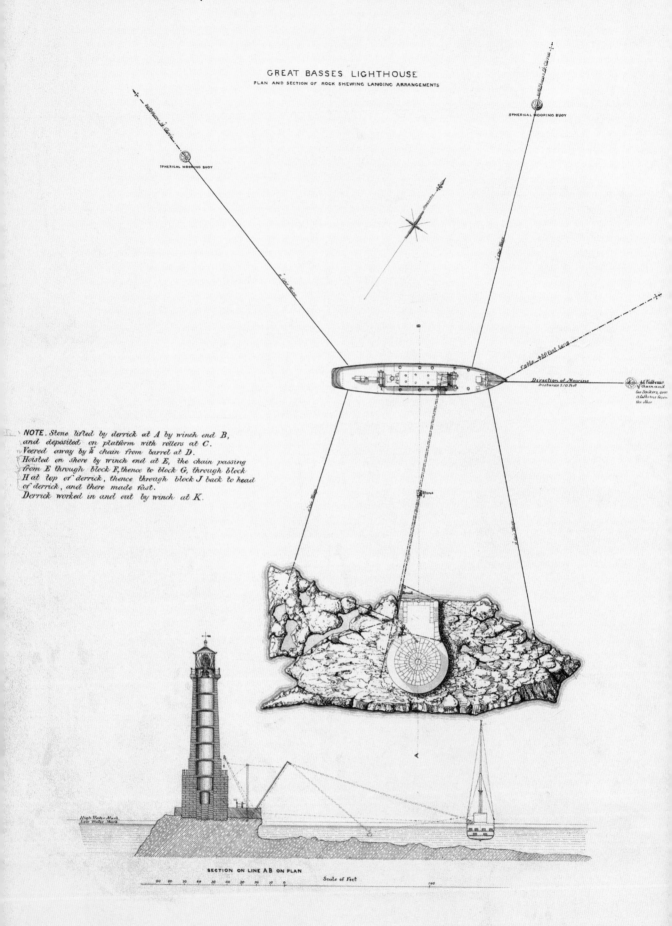

GREAT BASSES LIGHTHOUSE
PLAN AND SECTION OF ROCK SHEWING LANDING ARRANGEMENTS

*NOTE. Stone lifted by derrick at A by winch end B,
and deposited on platform with rollers at C.
Veered away by ½ chain from barrel at D.
Hoisted on shore by winch end at E, the chain passing
from E through block F, thence to block G, through block
H at top of derrick, thence through block J back to head
of derrick, and there made fast.
Derrick worked in and out by winch at K.*

SECTION ON LINE AB ON PLAN

Scale of Feet

The British Board of Trade decided that a light was needed on the hazardous Basses Reef, 80 miles (128 km) off Sri Lanka, then the British colony of Ceylon. A first attempt to build an iron tower in 1856 failed. In 1869, Trinity House undertook the project, with James Douglass designing a granite lighthouse and appointing his brother William on-site engineer. Two steamships brought granite blocks from Britain to the reef, while a lightship served as a barracks for workers. An ingenious system (above) was created for transferring the massive blocks from the steamships to the construction site.

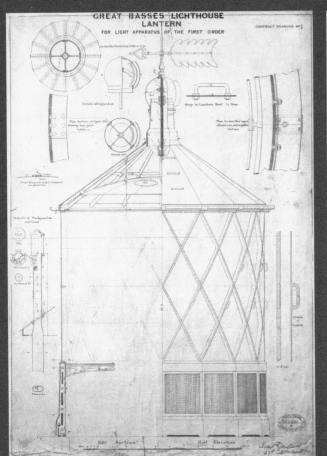

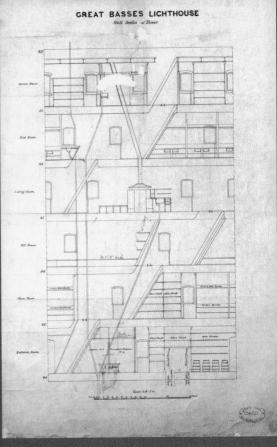

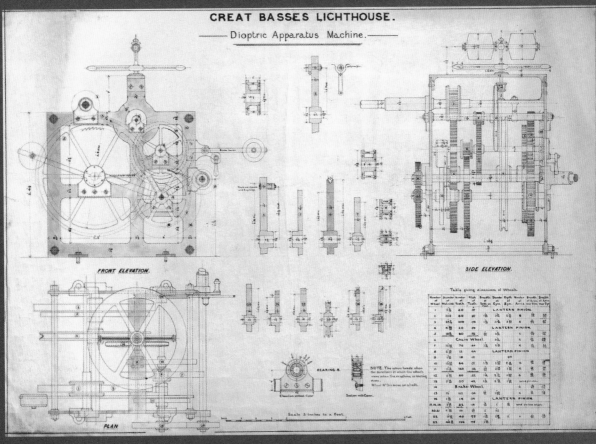

The first stone was laid in December 1870 and the light first lit in March 1873. The lantern (top left) was installed with the latest revolving lighting system developed by Chance Brothers of Birmingham, which delivered distinctive groups of rapid flashes. Its revolving apparatus required a complex mechanism (above). The interior of the tower (top right) included separate sleeping quarters and bathrooms for "natives" and European lighthouse keepers. The lighthouse was later fitted with a Chance hyperradiant Fresnel lens. It is still in service today.

133

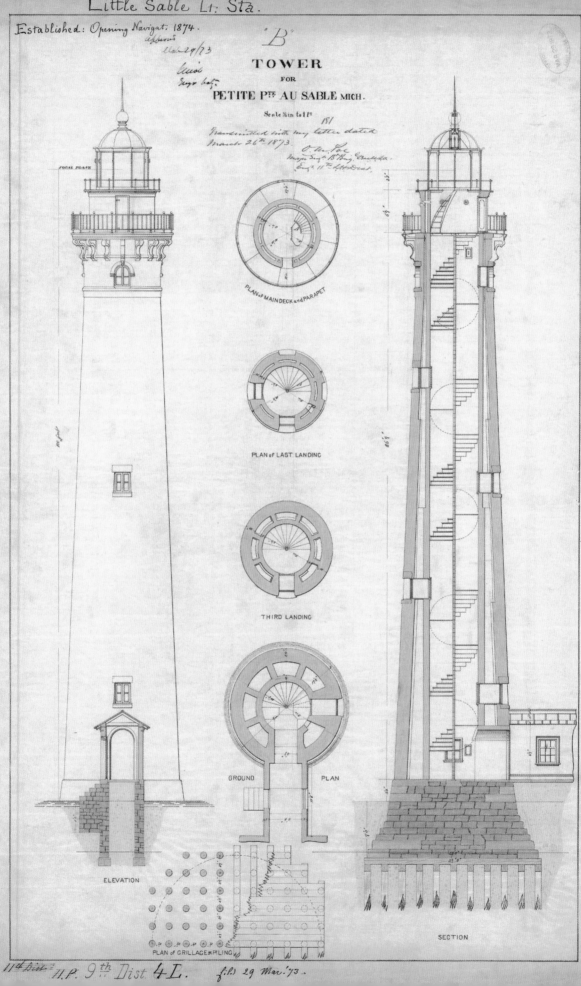

Little Sable Lt. Sta.

Established: Opening Navigat: 1874.

"B"
TOWER
FOR
PETITE PTE AU SABLE MICH.

Scale ⅛ in to 1 ft   181

Transmitted with my letter dated
March 26th 1873.

PLAN of MAIN DECK and PARAPET

PLAN of LAST LANDING

THIRD LANDING

GROUND   PLAN

ELEVATION

PLAN of GRILLAGE & PILING

SECTION

11th Dist. H. P. 9th Dist. 4 E.   f. P. 29 Mar.'73.

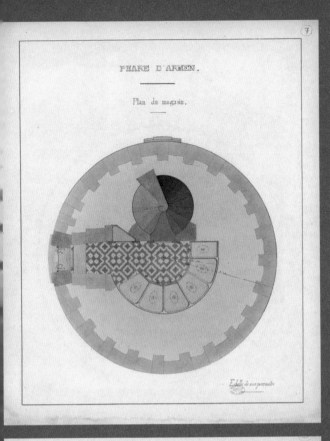

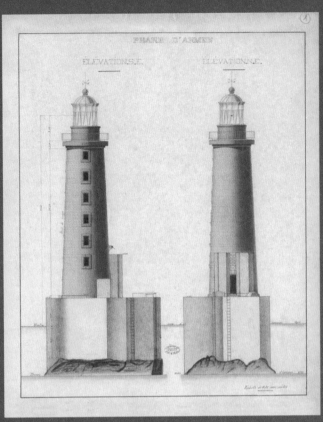

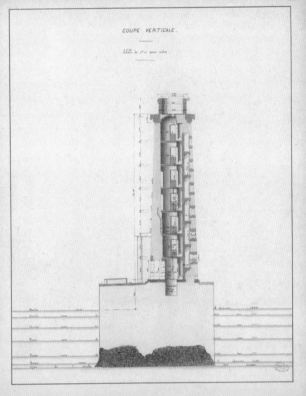

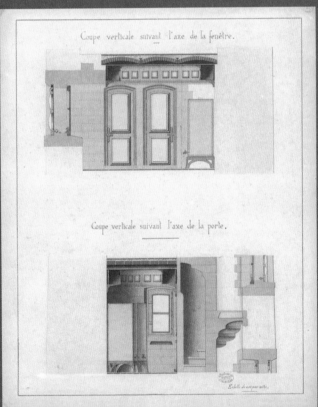

OPPOSITE Little Sable Point light was built on more than a hundred wooden piles driven into the shore of Lake Michigan. Construction began in spring 1873 and was completed the following year. A spiral stair with 139 steps rises to the lantern, which still contains a functioning Fresnel lens.

ABOVE The Ar-Men light stands on a rock in the Atlantic Ocean west of the Île de Sein. Its construction, which lasted from 1867 to 1881, was an epic feat of engineering. The granite tower rises from a solid base rooted in the rock with iron bars. It was extensively strengthened in 1897–1902.

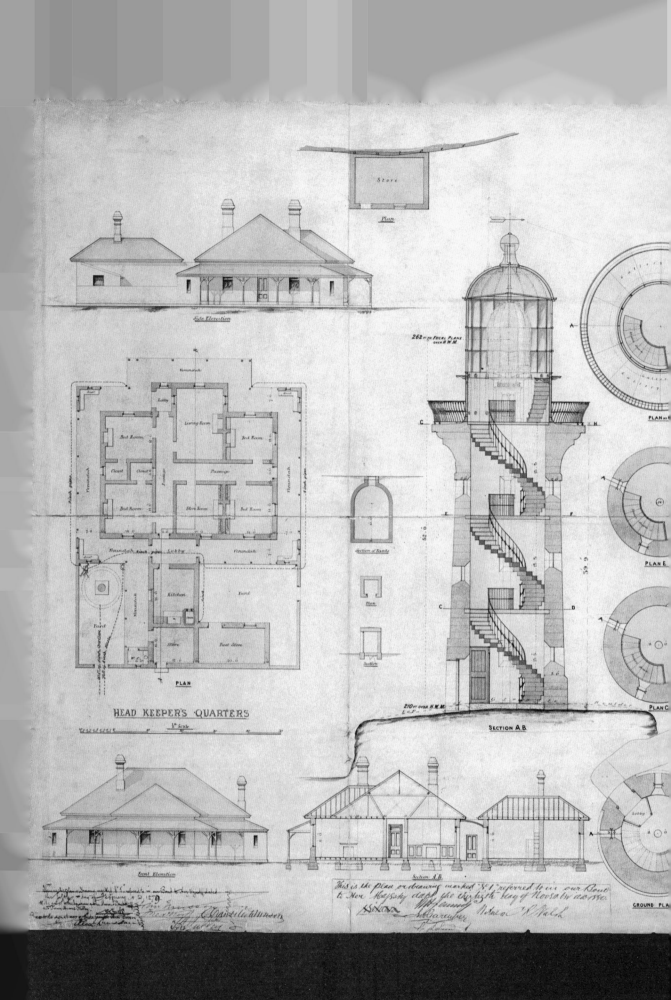

HEAD KEEPER'S QUARTERS

Side Elevation

Front Elevation

Section A.B.

SECTION A.B.

PLAN

Store

Plan

262 ft to FOCAL PLANE over H.W.M.

210 ft over H.W.M.

Section of Tanks

The decision to build a lighthouse on Montague Island off the south coast of New South Wales was taken in 1873. James Barnet, a prolific designer of lighthouses and other official buildings in New South Wales, drew up the plans. Various problems delayed the start of building work until 1880.

The light was lit in November of the following year. The tower is built of locally quarried granite hewn into dovetailed blocks. Single-story keepers' houses and other outbuildings were constructed around the tower. The original light is now on display in a museum at the nearby town of Narooma.

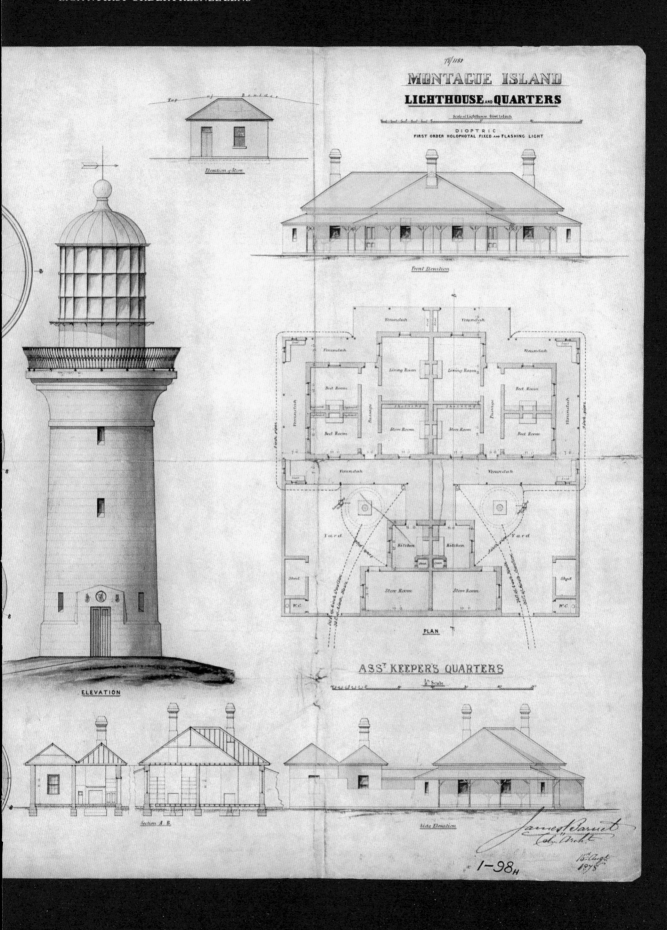

MONTAGUE ISLAND
LIGHTHOUSE AND QUARTERS

DIOPTRIC
FIRST ORDER HOLOPHOTAL FIXED AND FLASHING LIGHT

Front Elevation

Elevation of Store

Top of Boulder

ELEVATION

PLAN

ASS.T KEEPER'S QUARTERS

Section A.B.

Side Elevation

1-98ₕ

1885 ROTER SAND
WESER ESTUARY | GERMANY

DESIGNED BY **CARL FRIEDRICH HANCKES**
TOWER: **CAST-IRON CIRCULAR** | HEIGHT FROM
FOUNDATIONS: **172 FT (52.5 M)** | LIGHT: **FRESNEL LENS**

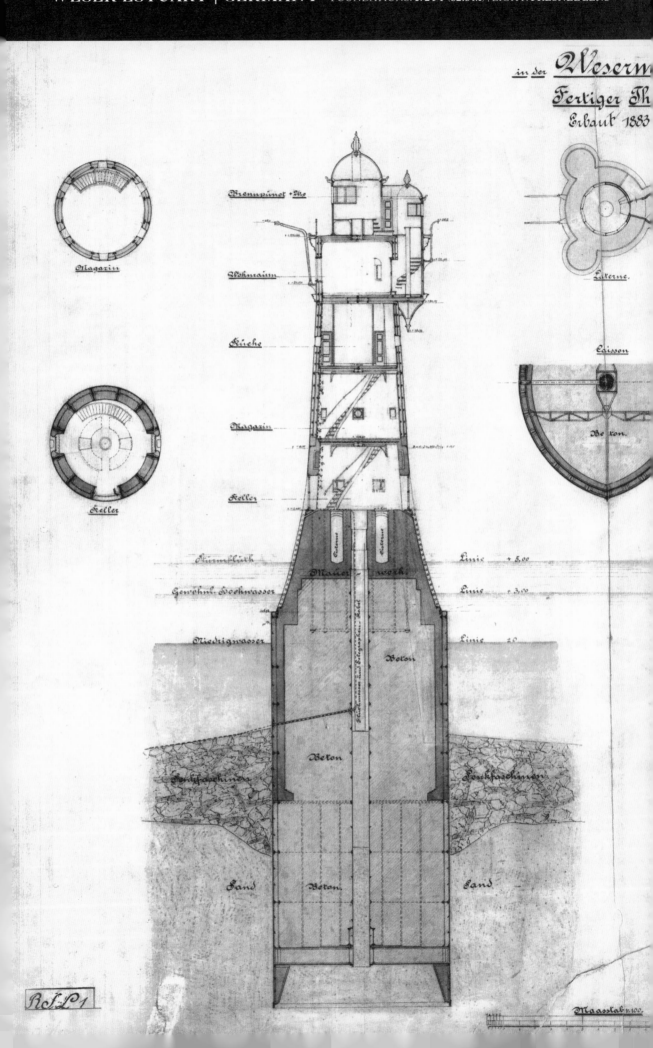

Oung.

Ansicht.

Sturmfluth

Gew. Hochwasser

Niedr. Wasser

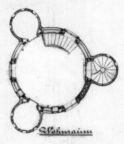

Wohnraum.

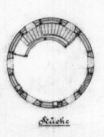

Küche.

Blitz Feuer
einblitzig

Ansicht
von
Oben.

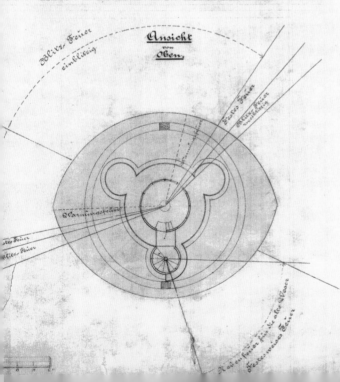

Der Oberbaudirector.   Der Kamrath.

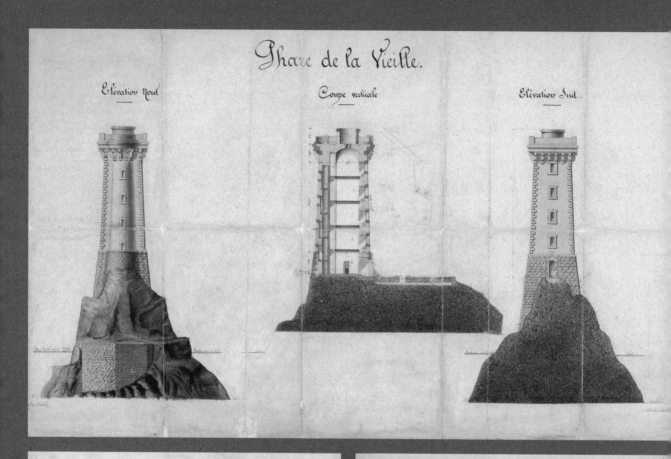

Phare de la Vieille.

Elévation Nord — Coupe verticale — Elévation Sud

PHARE DE LA VIEILLE

Elévation Sud

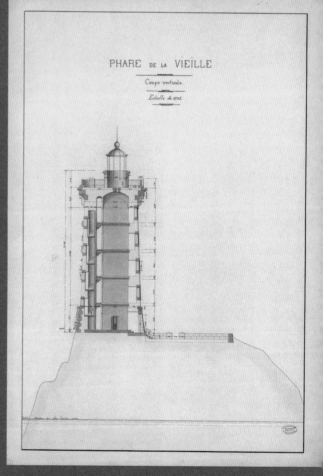

PHARE DE LA VIEILLE

Coupe verticale

Echelle de 0,01

The idea of building a lighthouse on the tiny island of Gorlebella off the coast of Finistère was first considered in 1861, but the task was initially dismissed as impossible. A tentative start on preparatory work was eventually made in 1879 and construction began in earnest in 1881. Made of granite and kersantite, the partially rusticated, crenellated tower reflected the 19th-century taste for a medieval look. The construction site was above the level of high tide, enabling work to progress at a reasonable pace despite the difficulty of access to the islet. The light was first lit in September 1887.

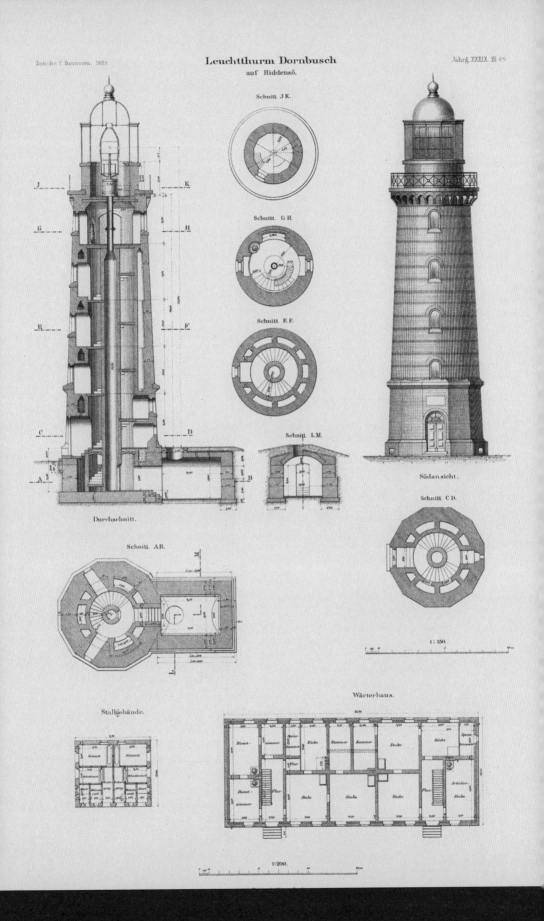

This lighthouse was built on top of the steep Bakenberg hill on the island of Hiddensee, off Germany's Baltic coast. The hill is covered in thorn bushes, hence the name of the lighthouse (which means "thorn bush" in German). The round

house was built separately. As the brick deteriorated under the influence of the weather, in 1929 the tower was enclosed in a twelve-sided cladding of reinforced concrete. There are 102 steps to the top of the tower, which is almost 328 ft (100 m) above sea level.

Élévation.   PHARE D'ECKMUHL   Coupe verticale.

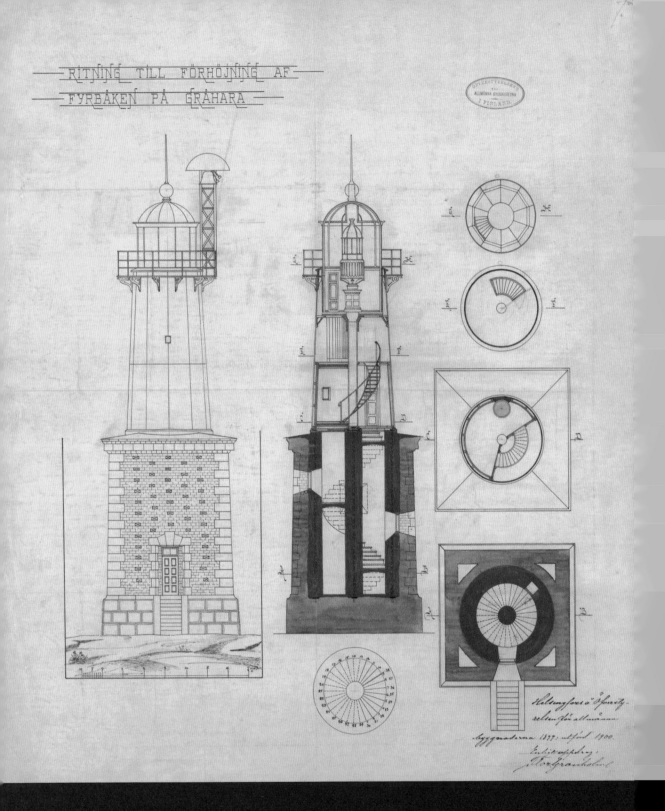

RITNING TILL FÖRHÖJNING AF
FYRBÅKEN PÅ GRÅHARA

OPPOSITE This lighthouse at Penmarch, Finistère, was
built with funds provided by a legacy from the daughter of
Napoleonic Marshal Davout, Prince d'Eckmühl. Built between
1894 and 1897, the tower has 307 steps up to its light room.
The lavish interior includes opaline glass tiling on the walls.

ABOVE Harmaja is a small island on the main ship channel
leading to Helsinki. A stone lighthouse was built on the island
in 1883, but it was too short and so was replaced by a new
tower in 1900. The interior of the granite and brick lower
half is round, matching the iron tower above.

Elektrisches Leuchtfeuer auf Helgoland.

Laterne des Leuchtturms.

Erbaut im Jahre 1902.

Vertikal - Schnitt.

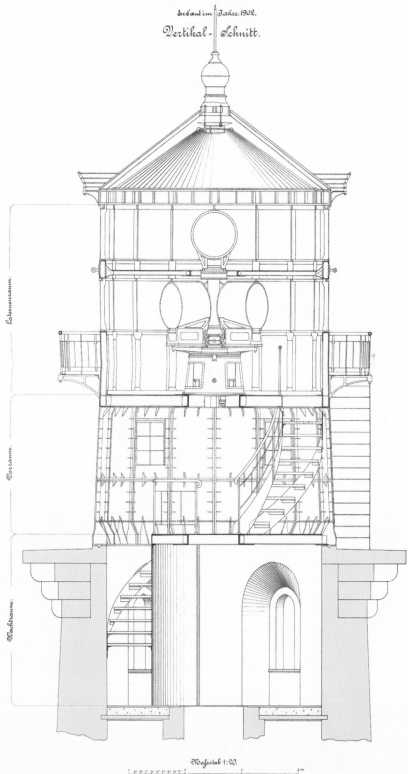

Laternenraum.

Vorraum.

Wachtraum.

Maßstab 1:20.

Wasserbauinspektion Tönning.

Inventarienzeichnung. Blatt. 6.

Elektrisches Leuchtfeuer auf Helgoland.

Anordnung der Scheinwerfer auf den drehbaren Plattformen.

Erbaut im Jahre 1902.

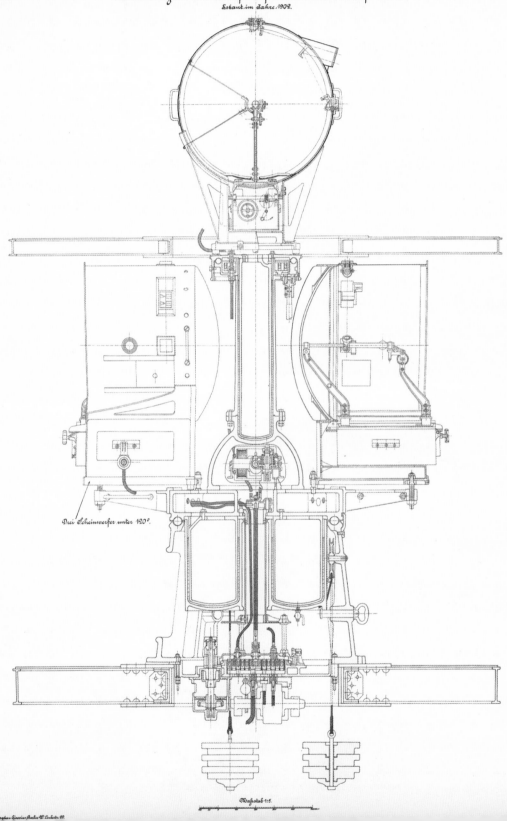

Drei Scheinwerfer unter 120°.

Maßstab 1:5.

Lith. Anst. v. Bogdan Gisevius, Berlin W. Linkstr. 16.

1907 CAPE PEMBROKE
FALKLAND ISLANDS

DESIGNED BY **THOMAS MATTHEWS** | TOWER:
ROUND CAST-IRON | HEIGHT: **70 FT (21 M)**
LIGHT: **THIRD-ORDER DIOPTRIC LENS**

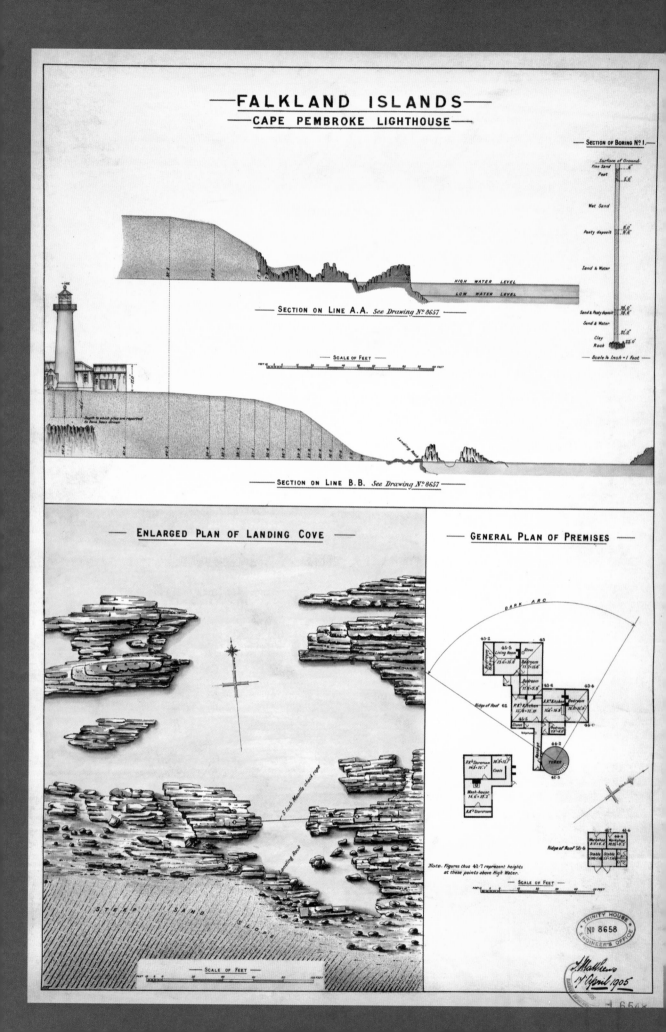

Trinity House established the first lighthouse on Cape Pembroke, some 7 miles (11 km) east of Port Stanley, in 1855. By the early 20th century, the foundations of this iron tower had become unstable. In 1906, work began on rebuilding the lighthouse on new foundations, with a more up-to-date lantern and light installation. These plans show both the old lighthouse (left) and the new (right). They also show the cove where materials were landed and the ancillary buildings around the tower. The lighthouse ceased functioning during the Argentinian occupation in 1982 but is now conserved as a museum.

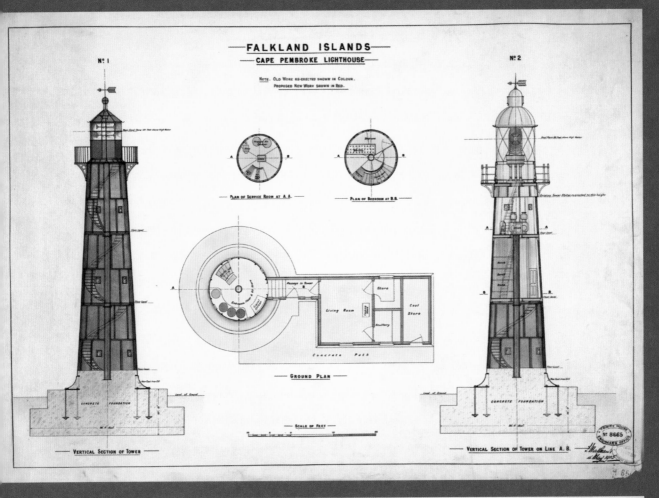

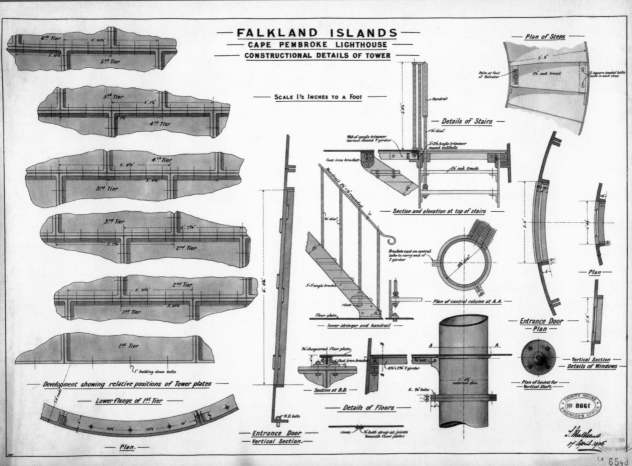

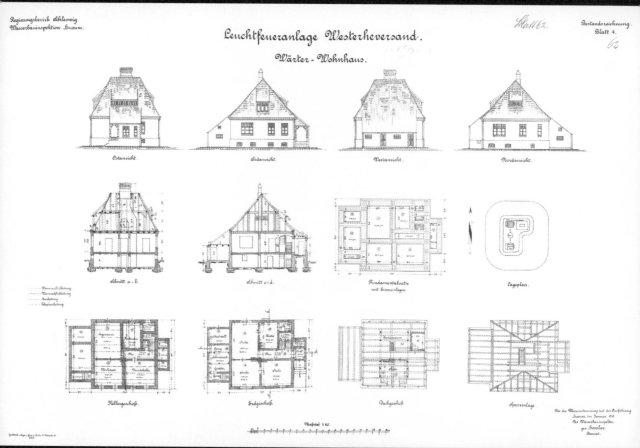

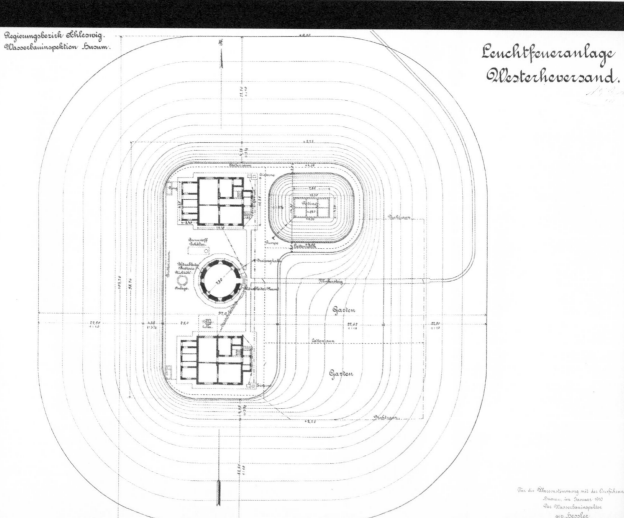

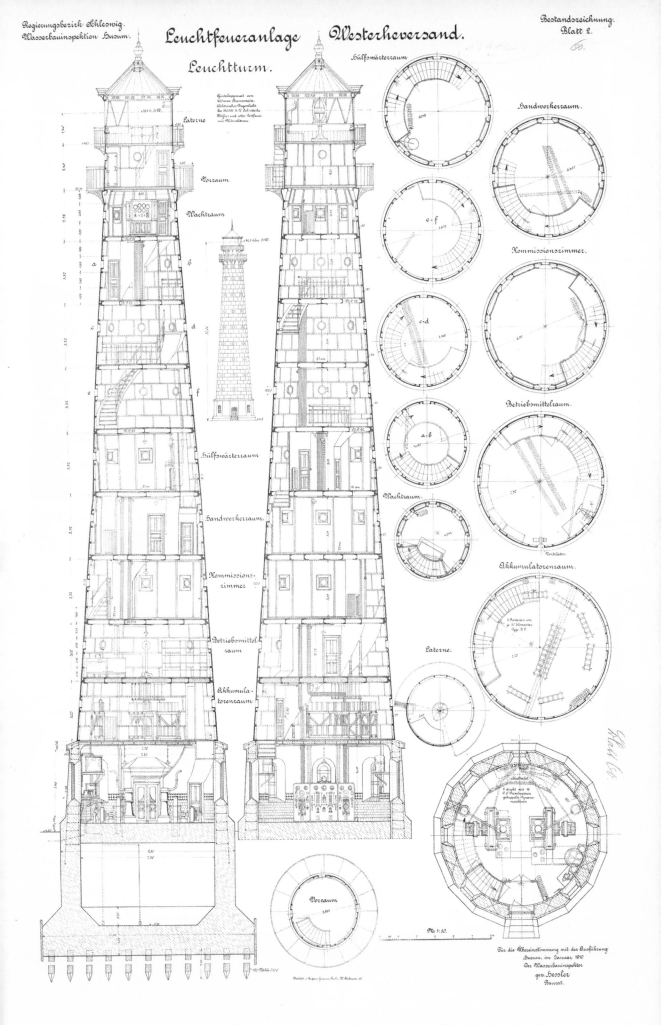

The famous Westheversand lighthouse stands on the Eiderstedt peninsula, on Germany's North Sea coast. Built between 1906 and 1908, it consists of a tapering iron tower, made from 608 cast-iron plates bolted together, rising from a concrete base. There is a double gallery around the lantern, which houses a carbon arc light. The electricity was originally provided by a diesel generator. The lighthouse building is flanked by two classic keeper's cottages (top left). One of these is now used as a register office, since the lighthouse has become a popular venue for weddings.

THE END

OF AN ERA.

1.

It was the middle of the 19th century, when US author Henry Wadsworth Longfellow wrote his acclaimed poem *The Lighthouse*, inspired by the Portland Head light (1791) in Maine. The poet lauds the light for its permanence:

> *Steadfast, serene, immovable, the same*
> *Year after year, through all the silent night*
> *Burns on forevermore that quenchless flame*
> *Shines on that inextinguishable light!*

But sadly, history shows that nothing is "immovable, the same," nothing is "forevermore." A hundred and fifty years after Longfellow wrote his poem, thousands of lighthouses across the world had been decommissioned, many had been demolished, and those that still functioned had been transformed into automatic beacons, deprived of the vigilant human presence that once gave them a heart and soul.

Change was driven by the practical imperatives that govern all modernization: efficiency, economy, and technological progress. Lighthouses were among the first locations to have radio installed. Guglielmo Marconi began experiments with ship-to-shore "wireless" transmissions at the South Foreland lighthouse (1840) in Kent as early as 1898. The Cape Race light (1907) in Newfoundland was famously in wireless contact with the liner *Titanic* during its fatal voyage in April 1912. From the 1920s, radio beacons were being added to the equipment of lighthouses, proving in some ways more effective aids to navigation than the light itself. Meanwhile, progress in electrification went hand in hand with automation; electric time switches and photoelectric devices provided an alternative to Gustaf Dalén's "sun valve" automatic control system. By the end of the 1930s, engineers were piloting the operation of marine lights by remote radio control. But the shift to automation was held back by a deeply ingrained suspicion of the reliability of untended machines. Writing in 1936, George Putnam, then recently retired as US Commissioner of Lighthouses, stated that for primary lights, in the interest of safety, "human attention, given by light keepers, must be retained." Thus, in the United States and much of the rest of the world, the majority of lights would remain staffed into the 1960s.

The traditions of lighthouse keeping did not remain static. The lighthouse families who felt they "owned" their

OPPOSITE

Top: North elevation of La Vieille lighthouse, Brittany.

Center left: 19th-century seal featuring the motto of the Northern Lighthouse Board, In Salutem Omnium ("For the Safety of All").

Center right: Gustaf Dalén in his laboratory. His lighthouse innovations included the Dalén light, the sun valve, and the Dalén flasher.

Bottom: Dalén's sun valve, which saves fuel by automatically turning off the lighthouse beacon during daylight hours.

ABOVE

Fig. 1.— Deserted lighthouse on Klein Curaçao island in the West Indies.

light became a dying breed as more impersonal, rationalized career structures evolved. Wars had their impact, too. In France, after World War I, a law was passed reserving posts as lighthouse keepers for disabled ex-servicemen, veterans of trench warfare. This policy was rapidly abandoned after two of these *mutilés de guerre* staffing the rock lighthouse of La Vieille (1887) off Finistère broke down under the pressure of the work and had to be rescued – with considerable difficulty given their poor physical condition. Tardily acknowledging that being a lighthouse keeper was a tough rather than a cushy occupation, the authorities repealed the legislation. During World War II, a number of the most famous French lighthouses, including Léonce Reynaud's celebrated Héaux de Bréhat tower (1840), were blown up by German occupation forces in a calculated act of vandalism in 1944. Most were lovingly restored in the postwar period.

2.

In the United States, the growing threat of another world war in 1939 led the Roosevelt administration to place lighthouses under the control of the Coast Guard, a part of the country's armed forces. At first most of the existing keepers stayed in place, many retaining civilian status, but increasingly they were replaced by young servicemen for whom lighthouse keeping was an arbitrary posting, and not necessarily a welcome one. Although English lighthouses remained as ever under the control of Trinity House, by the mid 20th century civilian keepers were rotated on a regular basis, allotted for spells of a few years to different lighthouses around the country. Keepers' families were provided with accommodation, whether at or away from the light, but they no longer worked the lighthouse as a family concern.

3.

There was a late reminder of the dangers and heroism of the lighthouse tradition in the United States' last major lighthouse tragedy shortly after the end of World War II. Five young US servicemen had been assigned to one-year tours of duty at the ultra-remote Scotch Cap lighthouse (1903) in the Aleutian Islands. In April 1946, the lighthouse was destroyed by a tsunami and all were killed. On the whole, though, major improvements were being made to the safety and comfort of lighthouse staff, just as their era was coming to an end. Radio allowed keepers at the most remote stations to remain in contact with the outside world, and also with passing ships. Television provided a source of entertainment to supplement the keepers' traditional books and hobbies. Refrigerators and

4.

Fig. 2.— *The radio station on the* Titanic, *in touch with a lighthouse radio during the liner's maiden voyage.*

Fig. 3.— *The 1940 Scotch Cap lighthouse on Unimak Island in the Aleutians.*

Fig. 4.— *Scotch Cap after its destruction by a tsunami in 1946.*

Fig. 5.— *From the 1970s, supplies and keepers could reach rock lighthouses by helicopter.*

Fig. 6.— *A pilot's view of the helipad on the Needles lighthouse, Isle of Wight.*

5.

6.

freezers solved the long-standing problem of food supply. By the 1970s, the use of helicopters was beginning to answer the ever-present problem of movement to and from the rock lighthouses. Elegant wave-swept Victorian towers ended up capped with helicopter landing platforms, to the considerable detriment of their aesthetic appeal.

By the time helicopters were serving lighthouses, pressure toward automation had already become irresistible. The Lighthouse Automation and Modernization Project (LAMP), initiated by the Coast Guard in the United States in 1968, provides a useful date marker for the process, but in truth automation was advancing piecemeal across the globe. At first, keepers stayed on to oversee and service the new automatic equipment. Then the job began to disappear altogether. In Britain, the Eddystone, the tower with which the golden age of lighthouses can be said to have begun in 1759, saw its last keepers leave in 1981. In France, the Héaux de Bréhat was automated a year later. The Portland Head light in Maine, celebrated by Longfellow, lost its last keepers in 1989. By the 1990s, Boston Harbor light (1716) was the only staffed lighthouse still functioning in the United States and it was automated in 1998. The last English lighthouse to be automated was North Foreland in the same year; the Northern Lighthouse Board also completed automation in Scotland in 1998. Kéréon light (1916) was the last staffed lighthouse in France, automated in 2004. Stubbornly, the Canadians clung to the old tradition with a few keepers in lighthouses on the Pacific coast. Here and there across the world, a scattering of resident staff survived as hosts for visiting tourists or as technicians operating sophisticated communications equipment.

Even in the world of radar and GPS, it was deemed beneficial to keep some of the lights lit, although the fog sirens were almost universally allowed to lapse into silence. What the future held for the lighthouses no longer considered useful, automated or not, was a question that concerned conservationists and local enthusiasts. Disused lighthouses should be valued and preserved, it was argued, as heritage, as history, and as architecture. This concern ran up against the realities of finance. Lighthouses would be too expensive to maintain, especially those in the most exposed locations, unless some means could be found to make them earn their keep. So lighthouses found a new vocation as attractions for tourists and day trippers, as museums, movie locations, and wedding venues. Keepers' cottages were turned into vacation accommodation. Oregon's historic Tillamook Rock light (1881) became for a while a columbarium, where you could pay to have your ashes stored in an urn. The Rubjerg Knude light (1900) in Jutland, Denmark, menaced with destruction by shifting sand dunes and coastal erosion, was turned first into a museum and then, briefly, into an art installation where a wind-powered prism created the effect of a giant kaleidoscope. Germany's well-known Roter Sand lighthouse (1885), rising straight from the seabed in the Weser Estuary, was a notable success for conservation. Switched off in 1964 and declared unsafe, the Roter Sand was restored after a popular campaign in the 1980s. It found a new lease on life from 1999 as a destination for day trippers and as a rough-and-ready hotel. People staying overnight had to accept that access to the lighthouse was limited by the weather, so they might have to endure an enforced prolongation of their visit if a storm set in.

In the British Isles, France, and many other countries, the original lighthouse authorities remained responsible for the conservation effort. In Australia, for example, by 2017 there were more than fifty heritage-listed lighthouses under government ownership. In the United States, surplus lighthouses were passed from the Coast Guard into the hands of local and national not-for-profit organizations dedicated to their survival.

Some lighthouse enthusiasts like to point out the potential fallibility of newfangled contemporary means of navigation, especially the US-controlled GPS. They ask whether the reliable old beams of light might not one day come back into their own. But in reality, lighthouses seem well on their way to joining other historic buildings as much-loved but non-utilitarian features of the landscape. And, like some historic buildings, it is quite possible that many will eventually survive only as romantic ruins. Yet a lighthouse without its light is a form without a function. It would be sad if future generations were never to see again, as Longfellow saw, how "…as the evening darkens, lo! how bright,/Through the deep purple of the twilight air,/Beams forth the sudden radiance of its light/With strange, unearthly splendor in the glare!"

7.

8.

Fig. 7.— The abandoned Rubjerg Knude lighthouse in Denmark was turned into an art installation in 2016.

Fig. 8.— Tourists visit the Roter Sand lighthouse in the North Sea.

Fig. 9.— The Stevenson lighthouse on the basalt rock of Dubh Artach still casts its shadow on the surf.

Overleaf— Abandoned cast-iron lighthouse at Whiteford Point on the Gower Peninsula in south Wales.

9.

SOURCES OF ILLUSTRATIONS.

Key to abbreviations: t = top, b = bottom, c = centre, l = left, r= right

2 Library of Congress, Prints & Photographs Division. HABS CAL,41-PESC.V,1-17 **4-5** (both) The National Archives, London, England. © 2017 Crown Copyright. MPH 1/274 **6-7** (all) New York Public Library Digital Collections **8-9** From *An Account of the Bell Rock Light-house,* published by Archibald Constable & Co., 1924 **10-11** (all) From *Report of the Commissioners Appointed to Inquire into the Condition and Management of Lights, Buoys, and Beacons,* printed by George Edward Eyre and William Spottiswoode for Her Majesty's Stationery Office, 1861 **12-13** National Archives of the United States, Records of the US Coast Guard, Record Group 26: Standard Apparatus Plans; Vol 9, Plate 98 **14** akg-images / Catherine Bibollet **16t, cl** From *A Narrative of the Building and a Description of the Construction of the Eddystone Lighthouse with Stone,* John Smeaton, printed by H. Hughs, 1791 **16c** Plymouth City Art Gallery **16crt, crc, crb, bl** From *A Narrative of the Building and a Description of the Construction of the Eddystone Lighthouse with Stone,* John Smeaton, printed by H. Hughs, 1791 **16br** From *Lighthouses and Lightships,* W. H. Davenport Adams, published by T. Nelson and Sons, 1871 **17** Courtesy Trinity House, London **18-20** (all) From *A Narrative of the Building and a Description of the Construction of the Eddystone Lighthouse with Stone,* John Smeaton, printed by H. Hughs, 1794 **21t, cl, cr** From *A Narrative of the Building and a Description of the Construction of the Eddystone Lighthouse with Stone,* John Smeaton, printed by H. Hughs, 1794 **21b** Universal History Archive / UIG via Getty Images **22tl** From *European Light-house Systems; Being a Report of a Tour of Inspection Made in 1873,* Major George H. Elliot, published by Lockwood & Co., 1875 **22tr** From *Lighthouse Construction and Illumination,* Thomas Stevenson, published by E. & F. N. Spon, 1881 **22c, crt** From *European Light-house Systems; Being a Report of a Tour of Inspection Made in 1873,* Major George H. Elliot, published by Lockwood & Co., 1875 **22crb** From *Lighthouses and Lightships,* W. H. Davenport Adams, published by T. Nelson and Sons, 1871 **22bl** *European Light-house Systems; Being a Report of a Tour of Inspection Made in 1873,* Major George H. Elliot, published by Lockwood & Co., 1875 **22brt** From *Lighthouse Construction and Illumination,* Thomas Stevenson, published by E. & F. N. Spon, 1881 **22brb** Relief representing the Roman lighthouse at Portus, Ostiense Museum, Ostia Antica **23** New York Public Library Digital Collections **24t** Mosaic representing the Roman lighthouse at Portus, Piazzale delle Corporazioni, Ostia Antica **24b** akg-images / Album / Oronoz **25** (both) Private collection **26t** Representation of the Tower of the Black Prince before the construction of the Lighthouse of Cordouan, circa 1590, by Claude Chastillon **26b** Bibliothèque nationale de France, MS 6439, RC-B-12216 **27tl, tr** From *Lighthouse Construction and Illumination,* Thomas Stevenson, published by E. & F. N. Spon, 1881 **27c** From *A Narrative of the Building and a Description of the Construction of the Eddystone Lighthouse with Stone,* John Smeaton, printed by H. Hughs, 1794 **27b** From *An Account of the Bell Rock Light-house,* published by Archibald Constable & Co., 1924 **28t** From *A Narrative of the Building and a Description of the Construction of the Eddystone Lighthouse with Stone,* John Smeaton, printed by H. Hughs, 1794 **28c** From *An Account of the Bell Rock Light-house,* published by Archibald Constable & Co., 1924 **28b** From *Lighthouse Construction and Illumination,* Thomas Stevenson, published by E. & F. N. Spon, 1881 **29** (all) Oldtime / Alamy Stock Photo **31t** © Mary Evans Picture Library **31c** Library of Congress, Illus. in AP2.N4 [General Collections] Copy 2 **31b** AR Collection / Alamy Stock Photo **32t** Courtesy Boston Public Library **32b** Library of Congress, LC-DIG-ppmsca-09661 **33t** Library of Congress, LC-DIG-ppmsca-09353 **33b** Ecole Nationale des Ponts et Chaussées, FOL.2110 **34t** PSF Collection / Alamy Stock Photo **34c** Private collection **34c, 35** (both) akg-images / arkivi **36** akg-images / Album / Oronoz **37** (all) From *Investigaciones sobre la fundación y fábrica de la Torre Llamada de Hércules,* Joseph Cornide, 1792 **38-39** Service Historique de la Defense **40** The National Archives, London, England. © 2017 Crown Copyright. MPI 1/455 **41** (both) © Bibliothèque nationale de France **42** National Archives of Sweden, Stockholm **43** Military Archives of Sweden, Stockholm **44** Service Historique de la Defense **45** (all) From *An Account of the Bell Rock Light-house,* published by Archibald Constable & Co., 1924 **46t** The National Archives, London, England. © 2017 Crown Copyright. MPG 1/894 **46b** The National Archives, London, England. © 2017 Crown Copyright. MPG 1/558 **47** Courtesy Trinity House, London **48l** Architekturmuseum, Technical University Berlin; 8109,10 **48r** Architekturmuseum, Technical University Berlin; 8109,09 **49** The National Archives, London, England. © 2017 Crown Copyright. RAIL 1057/3540 **50-51** (all) The National Archives, London, England. © 2017 Crown Copyright. MPH 1/274 **52-53** (all) From *An Account of the Bell Rock Light-house,* published by Archibald Constable & Co., 1924 **54-55** (all) From *An Account of the Bell Rock Light-house,* published by Archibald Constable & Co., 1924 **56t, ct** From *Lightships and Lighthouses,* Fredrick A. Talbot, published by W. Heinemann, 1913 **56c** Niday Picture Library / Alamy Stock Photo **56cb, b, 57t** From *Lightships and Lighthouses,* Fredrick A. Talbot, published by W. Heinemann, 1913. By permission of the Lighthouse Literature Mission **57c** Niday Picture Library / Alamy Stock Photo **57b** From *Lightships and Lighthouses,* Fredrick A. Talbot, published by W. Heinemann, 1913 **58t** From *Lightships and Lighthouses,* Fredrick A. Talbot, published by W. Heinemann, 1913. By permission of the Lighthouse Literature Mission **58c** From *Lightships and Lighthouses,* Fredrick A. Talbot, published by W. Heinemann, 1913. By courtesy of Lieut.-Col. W. P. Anderson **58b** From *Lightships and Lighthouses,* Fredrick A. Talbot, published by W. Heinemann, 1913 **59** (all) From *Lightships and Lighthouses,* Fredrick A. Talbot, published by W. Heinemann, 1913. By courtesy of *Scientific American* **60tl, tr, cl, cr** From *Puentes de hierro económicos, muelles y faros sobre palizadas y pilotes mecánicos,* José Eugenio Ribera, published by Librería Editorial de Bailly-Bailliere e Hijos, 1895 **60b** From *Lighthouse Construction and Illumination,* Thomas Stevenson, published by E. & F. N. Spon, 1881 **61t** From *Lightships and Lighthouses,* Fredrick A. Talbot, published by W. Heinemann, 1913 **61c** National Archives of the United States, 26-LG-69-55 **61b** Niday Picture Library / Alamy Stock Photo **62** Courtesy US Coast Guard **63tl, tr** From *Lightships and Lighthouses,* Fredrick ATalbot, published by W. Heinemann, 1913. Photo by permission of Messrs. Bullivant & Co., Ltd **63b** From *The Book of Knowledge,* published by The Grolier Society, 1911 **64-65** (all) The National Archives, London, England. © 2017 Crown Copyright. MPH 1/642 **66** National Archives of Norway, Oslo **67** Bibliothèque nationale de France, V-5682 **68-69** (all) From *Account of the Skerryvore Lighthouse, with Notes on the Illumination of Lighthouses,* Alan Stevenson, published by Longman & Co., 1848 **70-71** (all) Courtesy Trinity House, London **72** National Archives of the United States, Special List No 5: Lighthouse Plans In The National Archives Arts **73** National Archives of the United States, Special List No 57: Lighthouse Plans In The National Archives Arts **74** Courtesy Trinity House, London **74-77** (all) Courtesy Trinity House, London **78-79** (all) The National Archives, London, England. FO 925/4517 **80-83** (all) The National Archives, London, England. FO 925/4521 **84** (all) From *European Light-house Systems; Being a Report of a Tour of Inspection Made in 1873,* Major George H. Elliot, published by Lockwood & Co., 1875 **85** Metropolitan Museum of Art, New York. Gift of Janos Scholz, 1954 (54.632.2) **86tl, tr** From *Account of the Skerryvore Lighthouse, with Notes on the Illumination of Lighthouses,* Alan Stevenson, published by Longman & Co., 1848 **86c** Library of Congress, LC-DIG-ppmsca-09388 **86b** Library of Congress, LC-DIG-ppmsca-09389 **87** (all) From *Account of the Skerryvore Lighthouse, with Notes on the Illumination of Lighthouses,* Alan Stevenson, published by Longman & Co., 1848 **88t** From *European Light-house Systems; Being a Report of a Tour of Inspection Made in 1873,* Major George H. Elliot, published by Lockwood & Co., 1875 **88c** From *Account of the Skerryvore Lighthouse, with Notes on the Illumination of Lighthouses,* Alan Stevenson, published by Longman & Co., 1848 **88b** akg-images / arkivi **89** (all) From *Lighthouse Construction and Illumination,* Thomas Stevenson, published by E. & F. N. Spon, 1881 **90** Library of Congress, HABS CAL, 21-POREY, 1-8 **91t** From *Lightships and Lighthouses,* Fredrick A. Talbot, published by W. Heinemann, 1913 **91c** National Archives of the United States, 26-LG-6-6B **91b** Courtesy US Coast Guard **92** National Archives of the United States, 6281852 **93tl, tr** The National Archives, London, England. © 2017 Crown Copyright. MPG 1/936 **93b** The National Archives, London, England. © 2017 Crown Copyright. CO 48/229 **94-95** (all) The National Archives, London, England. FO 925/4519 **96-97** (all) Courtesy Trinity House, London **98-99** The National Archives of Finland (Kansallisarkisto), Helsinki **100** Musée maritime de Nouvelle-Calédonie, coll. J-C Estival **101** Mackinac State Historic Parks Collection **102** National Archives of the United States, 6-2T-14 **103t** The National Archives, London, England. © 2017 Crown Copyright. BT 356/455 **103b** The National Archives, London, England. © 2017 Crown Copyright. BT 356/455 **104-107** (all) The National Archives, London, England. FO 925/4518 **108** Courtesy Trinity House, London **109** (all) From *Minutes of Proceedings of the Institution of Civil Engineers, with Abstracts of the Discussions,* vol XXX, session 1869-70, Part II, published by the Institution of Civil Engineers, 1870 **110** National Archives of the United States, 5-4H-1-1 **111** National Archives of the United States, GA-3_2010_001 **112t** Historic Environment Scotland, SC781655 **112b** Historic Environment, Scotland, SC781665 **113** National Archives of the United States, AL-2_2010_001 **114-117** (all) The National Archives, London, England. FO 925/4516 **118-119t** The National Archives, London, England. © 2017 Crown Copyright. RAIL 1057/3540 **118-119bl, br** National Archives of the United States, PA-2_2010_001 **120tl** From *European Light-house Systems; Being a Report of a Tour of Inspection Made in 1873,* Major George H. Elliot, published by Lockwood & Co., 1875 **120tr** From *An Account of the Bell Rock Light-house,* published by Archibald Constable & Co., 1924 **120cl** From *European Light-house Systems; Being a Report of a Tour of Inspection Made in 1873,* Major George H. Elliot, published by Lockwood & Co., 1875 **120c** Courtesy Victorian Picture Library **120cr** Granger Historical Picture Archive / Alamy Stock Photo **120bl** From *Account of the Skerryvore Lighthouse, with Notes on the Illumination of Lighthouses,* Alan Stevenson, published by Longman & Co., 1848 **120br** From *A Narrative of the Building and a Description of the Construction of the Eddystone Lighthouse with Stone,* John Smeaton, printed by H. Hughs, 1794 **121** akg-images / Sputnik **122-123** (all) From *An Account of the Bell Rock Light-house,* published by Archibald Constable & Co., 1924 **124** (both) From *An Account of the Bell Rock Light-house,* published by Archibald Constable & Co., 1924 **125** Heinrich Hoffmann / ullstein bild via Getty Images **126** (all) From *Lightships and Lighthouses,* Fredrick A. Talbot, published by W. Heinemann, 1913. By permission of *Syren and Shipping* **127t, b** Gaston Paris / Roger Viollet / Getty Images **127c** George Konig / Keystone Features / Getty Images **128t** Private collection **128c** *View of the Interior of Longstone Lighthouse, Fern Islands, Grace Darling and her parents administering to the unfortunate survivors Saved from the wreck of The 'Forfarshire' Steam Packet on the 7th September, 1838* by H.P. Parker **128b** Photograph of Ida Lewis, 1869. Photographer unknown **129t** The Wreck of the Daniel Steinmann, Sambro Island Light, published in *Harper's Weekly,* 1884 **129c** Courtesy Maine Historical Society **129b** Courtesy Maine State Museum (82.6.63). Photographer unknown **130t** Private collection **130b** Photograph of Flannan Isle lighthouse keepers, c. 1900. Photographer unknown **132-133** (all) Courtesy Trinity House, London **134** Mackinac State Historic Parks Collection **135tl** Finistère Departmental Archives, 25 S 655 6 **135tr** Finistère Departmental Archives, 25 S 655 2 **135bl** Finistère Departmental Archives, 25 S 655 4 **135br** Finistère Departmental Archives, 25 S 655 7 **136-137** National Archives of Australia **138-139** Courtesy Förderverein Leuchtturm Roter Sand eV **140t** Finistère Departmental Archives, 25 S 768 4 **140bl** Finistère Departmental Archives, 25 S 768 1 **140br** Finistère Departmental Archives, 25 S 768 2 **141** Architekturmuseum, Technical University Berlin; ZFB 39,065 **142** Finistère Departmental Archives, 26 S 361 1 **143** National Archives of Finland, Helsinki **144** Architekturmuseum, Technical University Berlin; BZ-1 14,065 **145** Architekturmuseum, Technical University Berlin; BZ-1 14,066 **146-147** (all) The National Archives, London, England. © 2017 Crown Copyright. BT 356/346 **148t** Architekturmuseum, Technical University Berlin; BZ-1 22,062 **148b** Architekturmuseum, Technical University Berlin; BZ-1 22,059 **149** Architekturmuseum, Technical University Berlin; BZ-1 22,060 **150t** Finistère Departmental Archives, 25 s 768 3 **150cl** From *Lighthouse Construction and Illumination,* Thomas Stevenson, published by E. & F. N. Spon, 1881 **150cr** ullstein bild / ullstein bild via Getty Images **150b** Private collection **151** Frans Sellies / Getty Images **152t** Pictorial Press Ltd / Alamy Stock Photo **152c** Courtesy US Coast Guard **152b** Private collection **153t** Daniel Rowledge / Alamy Stock Photo **153b** Kos Picture Source Ltd / Alamy Stock Photo **154t** © Janjan Architects **154b** DDP / DAPD **155** Ian Cowe / Alamy Stock Photo **156-157** Rick Bowden / Loop Images / Getty Images **160** © Archives nationales, CP F/14/17515/1/6

REFERENCES.

PROLOGUE
'...the rock being so hard...' quoted in Adam Hart-Davis and Emily Troscianko, *Henry Winstanley and the Eddystone Lighthouse*, Sutton Publishing, Stroud, Gloucestershire, 2002; p.132

'...it was eleven days before...' quoted in Adam Hart-Davis and Emily Troscianko, *Henry Winstanley and the Eddystone Lighthouse*, Sutton Publishing, Stroud, Gloucestershire, 2002; p.142

'...stand forever as one...' quoted in Christopher Nicholson, *Rock Lighthouses of Britain*, Whittles Publishing, Dunbeath, Caithness, 2006; p.23

'...the greatest storm that ever was' quoted in Christopher Nicholson, *Rock Lighthouses of Britain*, Whittles Publishing, Dunbeath, Caithness, 2006; p.24

'...is broad at its base...' quoted in Christopher Nicholson, *Rock Lighthouses of Britain*, Whittles Publishing, Dunbeath, Caithness, 2006; p.32

'...very strong and bright...' quoted in Christopher Nicholson, *Rock Lighthouses of Britain*, Whittles Publishing, Dunbeath, Caithness, 2006; p.35

WONDERS OF THE WORLD
'...beacons, marks and...' quoted at trinityhousehistory.wordpress.com/tag/1566
'...a raft of timber rudely put together' quoted in Christopher Nicholson, *Rock Lighthouses of Britain*, Whittles Publishing, Dunbeath, Caithness, 2006; p.63

DEFYING THE ELEMENTS
'...no systematic or intelligible...' Alan Stevenson, *A Rudimentary Treatise on the History, Construction, and Illumination of Lighthouses*, John Weale, London, 1850, p.27
'...fatal catastrophe of which...' quoted in Bella Bathurst, *The Lighthouse Stevensons*, HarperCollins, London, 1999, p.73
'...a scuffle might have ensued...' quoted in Bella Bathurst, *The Lighthouse Stevensons*, HarperCollins, London, 1999, p.84
'nothing can equal...' quoted in Bella Bathurst, *The Lighthouse Stevensons*, HarperCollins, London, 1999, p.93
'...our slumbers fearfully interrupted...' quoted in Christopher Nicholson, *Rock Lighthouses of Britain*, Whittles Publishing, Dunbeath, Caithness, 2006; p.194
'...a storm broke...' quoted in Christopher Nicholson, *Rock Lighthouses of Britain*, Whittles Publishing, Dunbeath, Caithness, 2006; p.194
'...high up prisoned...' Robert Louis Stevenson, *Memories and Portraits*, 1887
'...an eggshell painted red...' quoted at www.lighthousefriends.com, Minot's Ledge MA

A LIGHT IN THE DARKNESS
'...sources of danger...' Frederick A. Talbot, *Lightships and Lighthouses*, William Heinemann, London, 1913, p.60

KEEPERS OF THE LIGHT
R. L. Stevenson, *The Light-Keeper*, quoted in Elinor De Wire, *Guardians of the Lights: Stories of U.S. Lighthouse Keepers*, Pineapple Press, Sarasota, Florida, 1995; p.32
'The lamps shall be kept...' 'Instructions for the Lightkeepers of the Northern Lighthouses', in Appendix to Alan Stevenson, *A Rudimentary Treatise on the History, Construction, and Illumination of Lighthouses*, John Weale, London, 1850
'...possessed of the strictest notions' Quoted in Bella Bathurst, *The Lighthouse Stevensons*, HarperCollins, London, 1999; p.97
'The process of landing...' David Stevenson, *Lighthouses*, Adam and Charles Black, Edinburgh, 1864; p.110
'...polish or otherwise cleanse...' 'Instructions for the Lightkeepers of the Northern Lighthouses', in Appendix to Alan Stevenson, *A Rudimentary Treatise on the History, Construction, and Illumination of Lighthouses*, John Weale, London, 1850
'...bane of a lighthouse keeper's life' Quoted in Ray Jones, *The Lighthouse Encyclopedia: The Definitive Reference*, Globe Pequot Press, Guilford, Connecticut, 2013; p.41
'A maiden gentle...' William Wordsworth, *Grace Darling*, 1843
'...if the lightkeepers were...' David Stevenson, *Lighthouses*, Adam and Charles Black, Edinburgh, 1864; p.116
'Quick the prow...' Benjamin Franklin, *The Lighthouse Tragedy*, found at www. newenglandlighthouses.net
'The life of a lighthouse keeper...' W. H. Davenport Adams, *Lighthouses and Lightships: A Descriptive and Historical Account of their Mode of Construction and Organization*, Nelson and Sons, London, 1870; p.276
'...night after night amid...' David Stevenson, *Lighthouses*, Adam and Charles Black, Edinburgh, 1864; p.114

SOURCES.

W. H. Davenport Adams, *Lighthouses and Lightships: A Descriptive and Historical Account of their Mode of Construction and Organization*, Nelson and Sons, London, 1870

Elinor De Wire, *Guardians of the Lights: Stories of U.S. Lighthouse Keepers*, Pineapple Press, Sarasota, Florida, 1995

Frederick A. Talbot, *Lightships and Lighthouses*, William Heinemann, London, 1913

David Stevenson, *Lighthouses*, Adam and Charles Black, Edinburgh, 1864

Toby Chance and Peter Williams, *Lighthouses: The Race to Illuminate the World*, New Holland Publishers, London, 2008

Adam Hart-Davis and Emily Troscianko, *Henry Winstanley and the Eddystone Lighthouse*, Sutton Publishing, Stroud, Gloucestershire, 2002

Tony Parker, *Lighthouse*, Eland Publishing, London, 1986

Bella Bathurst, *The Lighthouse Stevensons*, HarperCollins, London, 1999

Douglas B. Hague and Rosemary Christie, *Lighthouses: Their Architecture, History and Archaeology*, Gomer Press, Wales, 1975

Alan Stevenson, *A Rudimentary Treatise on the History, Construction, and Illumination of Lighthouses*, John Weale, London, 1850

Christopher Nicholson, *Rock Lighthouses of Britain*, Whittles Publishing, Dunbeath, Caithness, 2006

Ray Jones, *The Lighthouse Encyclopedia: The Definitive Reference*, Globe Pequot Press, Guilford, Connecticut, 2013

Cheryl Shelton-Roberts and Bruce Roberts, *Lighthouse Families*, Pineapple Press, Sarasota, Florida, 2013

John Naish, *Seamarks, Their History and Development*, Stanford Maritime, London, 1985

INDEX.

The publisher would like to thank Hester Vaizey and Timothy Cross and the Image Library at the National Archives, Kew, for making this book possible.

R. G. Grant is a historian and writer whose numerous publications include Battle at Sea: 3,000 Years of Naval Warfare, 1848: Year of Revolution, Commanders: History's Greatest Military Leaders and Flight: 100 Years of Aviation. He was also a significant contributor to the DK Visual History of the Twentieth Century. He lives in London.

Front-of-jacket and spine illustration: National Archives, Lighthouse at Cape Fear 1860, NA16285526. Back-of-jacket illustration: National Archives, London, England. © 2017 Crown Copyright. Coastline of Barbados 1855. MPD 1/8.

Published by arrangement with Thames & Hudson Ltd, London

Copyright © 2018 by Thames & Hudson Ltd, London

Text © 2018 by R. G. Grant

Black Dog & Leventhal Publishers
Hachette Book Group
1290 Avenue of the Americas
New York, NY 10104
www.hachettebookgroup.com
www.blackdogandleventhal.com

First published in the United Kingdom in 2018 by
Thames & Hudson Ltd, 181A High Holborn, London WC1V 7QX
First U.S. edition: May 2018

The Hachette Speakers Bureau provides a wide range of authors for speaking events. To find out more, go to www.HachetteSpeakersBureau.com or call (866) 376-6591.

Print book designed and illustrated by Anıl Aykan Barnbrook at Barnbrook

Cover design by Amanda Kain

Cover copyright © 2018 by Hachette Book Group, Inc.

Library of Congress Control Number: 2017955443
ISBNs: 978-0-3164-1447-0
Printed in China
10 9 8 7 6 5 4 3 2 1

The National Archives is the official archives and publisher for the UK Government, and for England and Wales. We work to bring together and secure the future of the public record, both digital and physical, for future generations. Many of our most popular records are available online: nationalarchives.gov.uk